ROM HERE TO MATERNITY

4 1 0172351 0

FROM HERE TO MATERNITY

Pregnancy and Motherhood
on the Autism Spectrum

LANA GRANT

Jessica Kingsley *Publishers*
London and Philadelphia

First published in 2015
by Jessica Kingsley Publishers
73 Collier Street
London N1 9BE, UK
and
400 Market Street, Suite 400
Philadelphia, PA 19106, USA

www.jkp.com

Library of Congress Cataloging in Publication Data
Grant, Lana.
From here to maternity : pregnancy and motherhood
on the autism spectrum / Lana Grant.
pages cm
ISBN 978-1-84905-580-2 (alk. paper)
1. Grant, Lana. 2. Autism spectrum disorders. 3. Autistic
people--Biography. 4. Pregnancy in mentally
ill women. I. Title.
RC553.A88G744 2015
616.85'8820092--dc23
2014036695

British Library Cataloguing in Publication Data
A CIP catalogue record for this book is available from the British Library

ISBN 978 1 84905 580 2
eISBN 978 1 78450 025 2

Printed and bound in Great Britain

To my parents, for their unwavering love and support throughout the good times and the bad.
To my husband, Steven, for always having faith.
To my amazing children, James, Matthew, Daniel, Charlotte, Olivia and Harry. You are my reason for breathing and my biggest achievement in life.

Acknowledgements

This book started out as a presentation given to people in the autism community and their parents and carers. My journey to this point has not been an easy one. There are so many people who have touched my life and given me faith to keep going. Without these people I would still be looking for my tribe.

My heartfelt thanks go to the following: my mother, Maureen Carter, for being my advocate and best friend; my father, Anthony Carter, for teaching me the values that have given me courage for the battles I have faced; my husband, Steven Grant, for the endless love, support and cups of tea; my children, James, Matthew, Daniel, Charlotte, Olivia and Harrison for giving me the material to write this book and for being my reason to write it; the many caring maternity staff that have supported me over two decades: the Birmingham Communication Autism Team and especially Lesley Baker, 'the boss', for giving me the environment to flourish in; the young people whom I work with, their parents, carers and families for making my job so worthwhile; Wendy for teaching me what a true friend is; the fabulous Kathryn for her proofreading expertise; my 'Developing Doula' tribe and all the wonderful doulas out there.

Contents

PREFACE 9

Chapter 1   What is Autism and Why is it Different
            in Girls? 13

Chapter 2   Me and My Asperger's 19

Chapter 3   James 26

Chapter 4   Matthew 51

Chapter 5   Daniel 56

Chapter 6   Charlotte 63

Chapter 7   Olivia 73

Chapter 8   Harrison 102

Chapter 9   What Lies Ahead... Adventures of
            an Aspie Doula 135

APPENDIX 1   FIRST TRIMESTER TOP TIPS:
             WEEKS 10–12 145

APPENDIX 2   SECOND TRIMESTER TOP TIPS:
             WEEKS 13–28 151

APPENDIX 3   THIRD TRIMESTER TOP TIPS:
              WEEKS 29–40 PLUS 157

APPENDIX 4   LABOUR AND BIRTH TOP TIPS 162

APPENDIX 5   LET'S TALK ABOUT LABOUR AND
              BIRTH POSITIONS 165

APPENDIX 6   BIRTH WISHES (BIRTH PLAN) 169

APPENDIX 7   MY HOSPITAL BAG: WHAT TO PACK
              FOR LABOUR 172

APPENDIX 8   MY HOSPITAL BAG: WHAT TO PACK
              FOR MY POSTNATAL STAY 175

APPENDIX 9   MY HOSPITAL BAG: WHAT TO PACK
              FOR MY BABY. 177

APPENDIX 10   ADVICE FOR MEDICAL STAFF WORKING
              WITH PREGNANT WOMEN ON THE AUTISTIC
              SPECTRUM 179

APPENDIX 11   HOW MY AUTISM MAY LOOK. 181

APPENDIX 12   HOW LABOUR PROGRESSES. 185

APPENDIX 13   PAIN RELIEF FOR LABOUR AND BIRTH. 189

Preface

I decided to write this book to highlight the different issues that females on the autism spectrum face during pregnancy and birth. I received my diagnosis of Asperger syndrome when I was 38 years old. This followed many years of being misdiagnosed with various mental health conditions, including depression and anxiety. These conditions seemed to become magnified during my first pregnancy. Don't get me wrong, I had difficulties as a child and as a teenager, but as a pregnant female I came into contact with the medical profession on a regular basis. It's not their fault that they didn't diagnose me correctly – after all, this was over 20 years ago. Even now it's difficult to get a diagnosis if you're female, but back in the day it was impossible unless you had other accompanying difficulties. I had five children prior to my diagnosis and another child afterwards. While pregnant with my sixth child, the first one post-diagnosis, I eagerly searched the Internet for information relating specifically to autism and pregnancy. There was nothing. Every time my search highlighted 'pregnancy and autism', I would click on it in anticipation only to realise that most of the articles related to issues during pregnancy that could cause autism.

It appeared that I didn't have a peer group; I didn't have a tribe to relate to. I eventually gave up the search and decided that I would have to find the information for myself. This led to my passion for highlighting the difficulties that females on the spectrum face. Difficulties range from being appropriately identified and assessed to obtaining support, recognition and a peer group.

After I had my son, my sixth child, I felt quite indignant. Here I was with my diagnosis, which had brought me such relief, but there was no peer group available – at least, not one that I could find. I felt even more disconnected and isolated. I felt certain that I couldn't be the only female on the spectrum ever to become pregnant. This thought spurred me on to write this book, and my hope is that women who read it will not feel as isolated, anxious and confused as I did.

As I take you on my journey through pregnancy, labour and birth, I will describe how being on the autism spectrum impacted on my experiences. I'll disclose my trials and tribulations and offer some tips on getting through the rollercoaster of pregnancy and birth. I'll also offer some guidance for partners, family, birth supporters, midwives and medical staff. As part of the reflective process of this book I found myself thinking about what would have helped me in my pregnancies. In all of my pregnancies and labours I never had one person to provide consistency of care. I saw many different midwives but never gave birth accompanied by someone I had met before. For those of us on the spectrum it is *so* important to have a relationship with a key person whom we trust and who can support us when we are anxious. This was where I needed an advocate, someone who understood me and could articulate on my behalf. Although my husband was there, he wasn't that person. Many dads-to-be are too emotionally involved and don't feel empowered to intervene on behalf of their partner. They automatically hand over the reins to the professionals. As I thought about this, I researched the role of a doula and decided to undertake training to become one myself. Doula (pronounced 'doola') is a Greek word meaning 'woman servant or caregiver'. It now refers to an experienced woman who offers emotional and practical support to a woman (or couple) before, during and after childbirth. A doula believes in 'mothering the mother' – enabling a woman to have the most satisfying and empowered time that she can during pregnancy, birth and the early days as a new mum. The support is practical and emotional in nature but non-medical. For me, being a doula that specialises in supporting pregnant women who have autism is probably the perfect vocation.

Writing this book has been a journey of emotions, reflection and regrets. It has also been a journey that has opened up new opportunities and given me back some self-esteem and self-awareness. When I began to write, I felt like a character, a plastic person with no definition. I felt as though I was playing a role in my own life and not quite getting it right. Now that I have travelled this part of my journey, I feel more at ease with myself and comfortable in my own skin. That is not to say that I have all the answers. I don't. I still have days when I feel 'wrong in my skin' and more autistic than usual. The difference now is that I recognise those days for what they are: a day in my life, and not the whole of my life.

Chapter 1

WHAT IS AUTISM AND WHY IS IT DIFFERENT IN GIRLS?

Autism is defined as a 'lifelong developmental disability that affects how a person communicates with, and relates to, other people. It also affects how they make sense of the world around them'.[1] In essence, autism is a social communication difficulty that may or may not have accompanying learning difficulties. It is a spectrum condition and so it encompasses a whole range of individuals. These individuals will share the same set of difficulties, such as problems with social interaction, social imagination and sensory needs, but they will be affected in different ways. I have met hundreds of people on the autism spectrum, and every single one of them has been unique.

When I deliver training to school staff, I often describe the autistic brain as being like an Apple Mac operating system and the neurotypical (non-autistic) brain as being like Microsoft Windows. Our brains are wired differently and that's fine. I also use this analogy when working with

---

1   The National Autistic Society (2014) *What is autism?* Available at www.autism.org.uk/about-autism/autism-and-asperger-syndrome-an-introduction/what-is-autism.aspx, accessed on 16 January 2015.

young people on the spectrum. They quite like being the Mac because it's considered cool! Because of this different wiring system, we also have difficulties with organisation skills. These vary, of course, in each individual. When I was younger, my organisational skills were quite rigid. I had a place for everything, and everything was in its place. Now I am older and have more things to organise, I find myself so overwhelmed that I'm like a dog chasing its tail. I go round and round in circles not knowing which bit to organise first, so eventually I give up out of exhaustion.

Autism was historically diagnosed using the Triad of Impairments.[2] This involved assessing a person using the following criteria:

- impairment of social relationships

- impairment of social communication

- impairment of imagination.

In more recent times it has been recognised that differences in sensory sensitivities also play a key role in people on the autism spectrum.

If we look at the three areas of the Triad of Impairments in more detail, we can understand some of the issues that may affect a person with autism. They can find it hard to form and maintain friendships and relationships due to their social and emotional difficulties. This links in with impairment of

---

2   Wing, L. and Gould, J. (1979) 'Severe Impairments of Social Interaction and Associated Abnormalities in Children: Epidemiology and Classification.' *Journal of Autism and Developmental Disorders, 9* 11–29. In Wing, L. (1995) *Autism Spectrum Disorders: An Aid to Diagnosis.* (3rd ed.) London: National Autistic Society.

social communication. Many people on the autism spectrum have trouble understanding and processing language. They may also struggle to understand jokes and sarcasm, often having a literal understanding of language. For someone with problems in these areas, the social aspect of life can be very challenging. This can result in social exhaustion and a need to spend time away from people in order to decompress. When you throw impairment of 'imagination' (for example, social imagination and flexibility of thought) into the mix, things can become complex. Many people with autism have very rigid thoughts and behaviours. They can engage in black and white thinking and this can cause problems in a world where there are so many grey areas. Now let's add a sprinkle of sensory sensitivities and we are looking at a complicated mixture of difficulties.

So why is it so important for us to be aware of the differences that females on the autism spectrum may experience? It's important because society has an expectation that females are more sociable and more emotionally literate than males. If a female presents differently, she can be viewed as cold, aloof or just plain weird. This is society's problem, though, not the problem of the person with autism. How can we change society? By raising awareness.

Many girls with autism can be quite passive and compliant. Often, they observe and copy the females around them. They may not show any of their difficulties outwardly. This can lead people around them to believe that they have none. Early behavioural signs that may be present in males with autism may just not be there in females. This leads everyone to think that there is no problem and that the girl is just shy.

Let's concentrate on her male peer who is demonstrating challenging behaviour. For many girls their problems develop over time, which is why they may not be diagnosed with autism until they are in their teens or, as I was, in adult life.

So far, we have been looking out for a female who is possibly quiet, shy and compliant, but what else can we look for if we are using the Triad of Impairments as our guide? There is imagination and flexibility of thought. Historically, many autism professionals felt that people with autism lacked imagination. Over time more research has been carried out and this is no longer considered a trait of autism. Many people on the spectrum, male and female, have a fantastic imagination. Many females on the spectrum write beautiful, imaginative stories about enchanted worlds. The problem lies with *social* imagination.

People with autism have difficulty understanding and predicting other people's intentions. They struggle to imagine situations that are out of their own experience. This can result in high levels of anxiety and engaging in a narrow, repetitive range of activities that are familiar and therefore comforting to them. This is why people with autism love routine. Actually, most people – autistic or not – enjoy having regular ways of doing things. Society runs according to rules and routines and we start teaching them to our children from an early age. The difference is that people with autism find safety in their routines and can often resist quite strongly any attempts at alteration. This doesn't mean that people with autism have to live their lives never experiencing change – after all, if there is one certainty in life, it's the certainty that change happens. The important thing is for society to be aware that people with autism are not being difficult and demanding for the sake of it. They need any change introduced slowly and scaffolded well.

The other trait that is associated with people on the spectrum is our special interests, sometimes called obsessions. I will refer to them as 'special interests' because I think 'obsession' has quite negative connotations. People with autism find familiarity safe, which is why many have a special interest that they can turn to when they are feeling anxious. In my experience of working within the field of autism I have found that many neurotypical people think that these special interests are male orientated (like trains, dinosaurs, cars). This is why when a female on the spectrum has a special interest in fairies or princesses, they are passed off as just 'being a girl'. Many girls on the spectrum may well have a special interest in trains but just as many may have a special interest in the things we associate with the female gender. It is not what the special interest is that counts but the intensity of that interest.

In my case, I think pregnancy became a special interest. I went from someone who never really wanted children – as described later in the book – to someone who had six children and, truth be told, would probably have another one! I became hugely interested in pregnancy and I retreated into it as something that was familiar. The hospital routines and the physical changes all became comforting to me. This may also explain why my relationship with my second husband has changed. I am only able to focus on one thing at a time, so once I am pregnant and then have had the baby, I can no longer focus on being someone's partner. I am a mother and while my child is still hugely reliant on me that is all I can be. Physically, I can't be a sexual being while I am in demand by a small child. This is difficult for a partner and can have a detrimental effect on a relationship. I would advise that if you feel this is happening to you, recognise that it can become a problem if you don't communicate your feelings to your 'other half'. I found that I needed to discuss my autism with my husband and explain that this didn't mean that I didn't love him; I just had problems with switching roles. Unfortunately, if you don't discuss this as soon as possible, it can become something that places a barrier between you.

I would suggest that if you are reading this book before becoming a parent, then read it with your partner and discuss the problems you may have with the transitional roles. I have been with my second husband for 18 years and it has not been easy as we both find it difficult to communicate our feelings, but we are still together so that must mean something. After having our first child together we would often go away for a weekend, usually for a birthday or an anniversary. As we had five children at home with us, it was a much-needed respite. It was during those weekends that I remembered why I had fallen in love with him and how much we could laugh together. So, if possible, take some time away and remember why you are a couple.

Chapter 2

ME AND MY ASPERGER'S

So far we have established that the autistic spectrum is exactly that: a spectrum. Although many people are now more aware of autism, unless they have direct experience they often only know what is portrayed in the media. More often than not, the media show only the two extreme ends of the spectrum and leave out all those people in between. Throughout my career I have worked with many people who have met one person with autism so they think they know what autism is. They don't. They only know how that one person's autism affects them. Human beings are all individuals; this doesn't cease to be the case because someone has autism. We are still individuals with our own unique combination of genetic make-up, upbringing and cultural variations.

For many years autism was thought of as a disorder that only affected males. However, we are now becoming more aware that it affects females as well. However, the presentation in females, as I have already described, is usually very different. Not enough is known about autism in females to understand why the presentation can be so different, and much more research needs to be done in this field. Of course, research has been difficult when there were hardly any diagnosed females to use as a test group. I get the feeling now through my work that we are on the brink of exciting new times in the world of autism and females. When I first began working with females on the spectrum about ten years ago, diagnosed girls were few and far between. Fast forward to now and there are certainly more girls being identified and put forward for assessment. However, I come across many females who are still being misdiagnosed. There continues to be a lack of awareness of autism and females. It is my hope that through books like this and other women speaking out, awareness will be raised.

Unfortunately, the news that autism is not just a boys' club does not appear to be filtering through to the diagnosticians. I believe there needs to be a clear diagnostic pathway, not just for girls on the spectrum but for the diagnosis of all. Currently, there seems to be a floundering within the medical profession over which diagnostic tools to use. Some people are diagnosed after a comprehensive, multi-agency assessment but others can be diagnosed after only one appointment.

Many girls with autism are only discovered later in life, as I was, after going down the mental health route. Such issues can be anything from anxiety to eating disorders. More awareness is needed about how autism can present in females, and there should be a diagnostic tool specifically for females. Diagnosis of autism in females is incredibly difficult with only a male set of traits to work from. I spent a large proportion of my life feeling as though I was a spectator in life, on the outside, looking in. My hope is that this book will give validity to those females who identify as autistic and also support females who are diagnosed. More importantly, I wish to highlight how necessary a specific female diagnostic tool is.

Autism is a social communication difficulty, and this leads to particular problems for females on the spectrum since we are genetically programmed to be more social. There is also an expectation from society that girls are 'good' and boys are 'troublesome'. When I worked in a school, quite often the teachers were pleased if their class was girl heavy. It is this expectation that girls are more compliant than boys that can mask autistic girls' traits. Many girls with autism are quiet and withdrawn – I certainly was – and are classed as 'just shy'. The fact that this quiet, introverted nature may be a social communication difficulty is not recognised. Many girls I have worked with have such high levels of anxiety that they avoid asking questions in school because they don't want to draw attention to themselves. Just getting through the day places great pressure on many of them.

As I mentioned in Chapter 1, girls' as well as boys' special interests can be 'gender appropriate'. Girls may have a special interest in animals, history, music or soap operas. It is not the subject of the special interest that is important; rather, it is the intensity of the interest that identifies it as more than a hobby. I had special interests that ranged from stamp collecting to dance and music, I collected novelty soaps and I used to cut models out of catalogues so that I could organise them into families. My imaginative play was limited but my imagination was astonishing. I loved music – my father used to play guitar professionally, and music was constantly in our house when I was growing up. I usually played the same song over and over again until I knew all the words.

From an early age females on the spectrum may observe and copy female role models. My mother is very neurotypical and I would spend a long time watching her mannerisms and mimicking them in the mirror. I also watched a lot of films. I had a fascination with the actress and icon Marilyn Monroe. I covered my bedroom with posters of her, watched all of her films and bought any books I could find about her. I couldn't go a day without engaging in something to do with Marilyn. Now I have a box full of books about her in the loft that I never really look at. I watched a lot of soap operas too, especially *Dynasty* and *Dallas*, and I was convinced that this would be the life I would have as an adult.

As a child I was considered to be shy and quiet. I never spoke to people we met in the street and I can remember refusing to go to parties; and if I did go (because my parents thought that I needed to socialise more), I hated every minute. One particular party stands out to this day. My grandfather worked for the police force and every year they had a Christmas party. I must have been about seven years old and I remember standing on the outside of a circle of children as they took part in a party game. It was my idea of hell.

Another thing was my repetitive, ritualistic behaviours, which nobody was aware of as I kept them internalised. For example, I used to pray for my family at night; I had to say all of their names and if I got them in the wrong order I had to start again.

I ran away from primary school a couple of times but I think this was more about wanting to be at home with my mother than anything awful happening at school. I would say that I was probably overwhelmed on those occasions. Mostly I flew under the radar at school. I was the ghost child who flitted through the corridors not wanting to be noticed. I was mothered by some of the other girls at primary school and was often to be seen around the edges of groups. To the untrained eye I looked as though I was joining in but in reality I was just an observer.

Up until the end of primary school, I was pretty much a tomboy. I played football and climbed trees, and my gorgeous Border Collie dog, Shep, was my best friend and confidante. Instinctively, my parents knew that I would be lost within the local secondary school, which was a large comprehensive, so I was sent to a private girls' school. In one respect this helped because the rules and routines were rigid and the class sizes were small. On a more negative note, it was a school full of girls. The mothering relationships no longer existed and I struggled with the subtle social behaviours of my peer group.

At the age of 15 I still hadn't gone through puberty and I was painfully thin. I didn't have an eating disorder but I had always been what my mother called a 'picky eater'. My issues with food were nothing to do with being conscious about weight – in fact, I was desperate to pile on the pounds. My pickiness was more to do with sensory sensitivity to certain foods. I didn't know it then but I have since discovered that I am hypersensitive to smell, taste and touch. I couldn't wear clothes with labels or any of the nylon clothes that were so fashionable in the 70s. I had an aversion to the flocked wallpaper in our hallway and hated certain bed covers.

As I approached puberty, I had dreadful mood swings and feelings of disassociation. It was around this time that I became extremely unhappy. I was struggling socially with friendships and I was also quite immature. I listened to other girls in my year group talking about their sexual exploits and felt that I was missing out because I still felt like a little girl. I didn't begin menstruation until I was 16 and I hated my body, which still looked very much like a prepubescent girl's. Twenty years later I discovered that this feeling I had of not really completing puberty was linked to my struggles with breastfeeding.

At school I was predicted good grades and considered academically able. However, there were subjects that I struggled with – mainly maths. I hated it (well, most of it). I was excellent at algebra and rote maths, but when concepts such as geometry and spatial awareness were introduced, I just didn't get it. Try as I might I couldn't make my brain understand it.

The subject that I loved the most was drama. I am now aware that lots of people on the spectrum are good at acting. The best way to get through life is to pretend to be someone else. I excelled at drama and won many medals. These achievements, along with my love of dance, helped me to decide where my future would lie and I went to college to study for a drama and theatre studies qualification. Unfortunately, the change from private school, where everything was structured and rule-based, to college, where there was more emphasis on independent study, completely threw me. I began skipping lectures and hanging around with the wrong crowd. It was here that my relationship with alcohol became established. I realised that when I drank alcohol I became a different person. Other people liked this new person, I liked this new person… she was wild and confident. She was also reckless and out of control. This relationship with alcohol and my increasing unhappiness at not fitting in led me to embark on a lifestyle that was a road to self-destruction. I left college – well, I was asked to leave, something that I only recently confessed to my parents. Up until a year or so ago they thought that I had left college because I wanted to get a job to earn my own money.

I had a succession of jobs after leaving college. I was good at getting work as I successfully acted my way through interviews. However, I wasn't quite so successful at keeping jobs. The act was impossible to keep going day after day. I worked in retail, in offices and even at a dental surgery but I seemed to make a dramatic exit from each workplace. Either I became exhausted and depressed, or I had a misunderstanding with a work colleague and found that I couldn't face going back. I eventually found myself in London following a transfer from the company I worked for to one of their branches in the capital. I had always wanted to live in London. Its size and the fact that you could be very anonymous appealed to me. This was going to be my fresh start.

Regrettably, I fell victim to an overbearing man who eventually became my first husband and the father of four of my children. From the beginning of my adventure down to London I was pursued and eventually worn down. This appears to be a theme for some women on the spectrum. Our naïvety means that we don't realise who is a predator and who isn't. We don't pick up on the signals from men and quite often we are unaware of the signals that we ourselves give out, mainly because we have copied them without understanding their full meaning. My vision for the future in my work is that the girls that I support will learn those signs and will develop good self-esteem and resilience so they can be strong, independent women.

Chapter 3

JAMES

As a child and a teenager I never wanted to be a mother. I didn't dislike children; I just didn't have any particular fondness for them. However, I did have an aversion to pregnancy. I found it an interesting idea but not something that I felt I needed to experience. I didn't want my body taken over. I had seen alien films where extra-terrestrials invaded bodies and exploded out of them. This was my vision of pregnancy. It didn't help that my mother had told me how she had morning sickness all day for the whole nine months of her pregnancy with me.

I have a fear of vomiting.

She also told me that she spent the last three months of her pregnancy in hospital.

I have a fear of hospitals.

So as you can see, pregnancy for me was never going to happen.

Then it did.

My first pregnancy was a surprise, mainly to me. I had experienced some gynaecological problems from the age of about 15, and in the course of investigations I had been told by a doctor that due to the positioning of my cervix I would be unable to have children. I think that because I had been told I wasn't capable of it (even though it wasn't something I really wanted to do), subconsciously I was intrigued as to whether I could or not. A few months later I found out that the position of my cervix was not going to prevent me from getting pregnant. I began to feel different very early on in my first pregnancy and subsequently learned to recognise the early signs in all my other pregnancies. However, with my first pregnancy I simply knew that I felt strange. I put this down to the fact that I had come out of an intense but unhealthy relationship and fallen straight into another toxic liaison.

I had moved to London to a new job and was feeling homesick and vulnerable. I was still under the impression that I had an uncooperative cervix, so although I wasn't consciously trying to get pregnant, I probably wasn't as careful as I should have been. When I became pregnant, suddenly I was so tired that I couldn't get up to go to work. I constantly felt sick and also desperately hungry. I would crave certain foods – usually spicy things such as curry – but as soon as they were in front of me I felt nauseous and couldn't eat them.

Concerned that I was suffering from some serious and deadly disease (I've always had high anxiety levels!), I made frequent visits to the doctor. Unfortunately, this was the doctor who thought my cervix was preventing me from producing any offspring, so pregnancy was the last thing he was looking for. Eventually, I was referred to hospital for a colposcopy. I was terrified that I had a life-threatening condition so I asked my mum to travel down to London to accompany me. I got gowned up and went in. A colposcopy is a procedure where a camera is inserted into the cervix to look for any cervical changes. It was painless, just mildly uncomfortable, but once the camera was in place the doctor carrying out the procedure said that they would not be continuing as my cervix was indicating that I was pregnant. This news came as a complete shock as I believed that I wasn't able to have children.

My initial reaction was one of defiance towards the doctor who had told me that I had a laid-back uterus...not quite as laid-back as he thought! I have to say I did feel a surge of pride in my uterus for doing something it had been accused of being incapable of. My second reaction was sheer panic and an element of disbelief. I wasn't married and, in fact, I hadn't really known the father-to-be for very long. The relationship I had with him was quite overpowering and certainly not something I had envisaged as long term. He was a controlling character and I was very submissive in that relationship. This turn of events was not in my life plan. I also had my mum waiting for me outside. How was I going to tell her? There was a stigma attached to being an unmarried mother in those days. I felt again that I had failed at life and done something wrong. I decided that I wasn't going to tell my mum what the hospital had said (they were probably wrong anyway) and that I needed further confirmation. I got changed in a daze and left the room to find my mum. As soon as she saw me she could tell from my expression that something was wrong. She also jumped to the conclusion that I was very ill, so I had to tell her the truth.

It's one thing when your life plan changes and *you* struggle with change, but when the people you care about are disappointed and hurt because of that change, that makes it harder. My parents are amazing (my dad is definitely an undiagnosed Aspie and my mum, as I have mentioned, is very neurotypical) and I have a good relationship with them.

However, as a parent myself I can now see why they weren't exactly thrilled at the news of my pregnancy. I had recently moved to London and started a new job. This was supposed to be my fresh start. I was 19 years old and the father of my baby was someone I had known for only a short time and not someone my parents liked very much – they were right to feel this way about him but I only found out for myself after I had married him.

My initial feelings of pride for my rebellious uterus soon became feelings of terror about what lay ahead for me. There was no question in my mind that I was having this baby. I fell in love with it as soon as I processed the news. My concern was how I was going to cope and, more importantly, how I was going to get the baby out! I began to devour all the information I could find on pregnancy – no easy thing as this was well before the days of the Internet. I knew that I was pregnant even before a second test confirmed it, because my body felt so different. I developed dreadful travel sickness. One day I fainted on the tube on the way to work and had to be carried off, on a stretcher, in rush hour in Central London with commuters stepping around me. I was so tired I could never sleep enough. I would wake in a panic and a hot sweat, feeling desperately nauseous. I couldn't eat anything. I wasn't actually sick but the smell of food became overwhelming. I didn't have a diagnosis of autism at this point and I remember thinking that if this was what pregnancy was like for every woman, why did people ever have more than one child?!

My baby's father made hurried preparations for our wedding. I hadn't wanted to get married – my instinct told me that it wasn't the right thing to do. I told my partner that I would be returning home to my parents and that he could play a full role in the baby's life but I didn't want to be his wife. He was insistent though, and because I was pregnant and vulnerable, I agreed. The feeling of having let my parents down was massive and I thought that at least if I got married before the baby was born, that would be one less disgrace for our family. Looking back at my wedding photographs, I look so very young and scared.

After marrying and moving to live closer to my parents, I adopted the role of wife and mother-to-be. I now know that this was to become the theme of my life…playing a role. This is very typical of the descriptions from other females on the spectrum. We often act our way through life, and this comes back to the difficulties with social imagination. I had an idea of what 'good mothers' were like from my own mother, and also from television. I had watched a lot of 50s films and this was how I imagined married life to be. This was my reference point and where I got my script from. I was on a quest for perfection and *I* had to be perfect. This is also a common feature in females on the autism spectrum. If you spend your life watching and copying, then the images that you see are usually the ones portrayed by the media as being perfect and good. It is therefore a natural progression to expect that your success and happiness in life depend on you being perfect. We women on the spectrum watch and copy and subtly begin to mask our differences from an early age. I had a vision in my head of how my married 'grown-up' life was going to be, and it was very Doris Day.

As I have already explained, during my childhood and teen years I had been a picky eater with lots of sensory challenges. I was hypersensitive to certain smells, so if a food smelled a certain way to me, that would dictate whether or not I could eat it. I was also sensitive to textures and some foods would make me gag. In pregnancy I was still very sensitive but I was consuming much larger quantities than I usually did. I was extremely aware of any minor changes in my body. All my life, I'd been super-sensitive, and as many people on the spectrum report, I often felt that I was from another planet. This extra sense, as it seems to be, can be used in a very positive way. I would describe myself these days as an 'empath'. I can often tune into other people's feelings and I've always felt that this was something I'm good at. Unfortunately, when I was younger I was overwhelmed with emotions that I couldn't control. Now I'm older and have more self-awareness, I can harness those empathy traits and use them more productively.

I felt my baby's movements (bizarrely called 'quickening') for the first time when I was 14 weeks pregnant. This may well have been partly because I was incredibly slim (I weighed only six stone) due to my difficulties around food. It was the most wonderful feeling, like a butterfly dancing in my tummy. I desperately wanted to see what was going on inside my womb. For me this is the worst part of pregnancy on account of the waiting. By 12 weeks I hadn't even been to the hospital. I had all this activity going on inside me yet life was continuing as normal.

When I did attend the hospital for the first time, it was exciting but terrifying. The overwhelming smells and noises were hard to deal with. Unfortunately, maternity care was not like it is in films. I was part of a conveyor belt where I would go in and be weighed (my weight shouted out for everyone to hear); then I was told to produce a urine sample. I was handed a bottle with white powder in it and no instructions other than to pee into it. So what did I do with the powder? Did I leave it in when I peed? Did I empty it out, then pee? Did I wash it out with water, then pee? Too many questions, and by this time I was hot and panicky. I didn't want to go and ask in case people would think I was stupid. This was one of many difficulties I encountered whilst dealing with medical staff. For them the various procedures are everyday occurrences. Most neurotypical women would probably ask what to do but for women on the spectrum such situations are overwhelming.

In the end I peed into the powder and said nothing. To this day I don't know if this was the right thing to do (I did the same with each pregnancy!). After filling my pot I had to leave it on a shelf in the toilet. Mass panic. I sat with sweaty palms wondering if they would get my sample mixed up with someone else's. Every single time I went to the hospital, I went through the same experience. I would do my sample, leave it in the toilet and then sit watching the toilet door with an incessant internal dialogue going on in my head. I had my first five children in the same hospital and my sixth child in a different one. It was the same in both places: pee bottles with powder in and no instructions as to what to do with the powder; leave your sample in the toilet and someone collects it. This has got to be a system where mistakes are waiting to happen. By the time I got to my fourth child at least they had stopped weighing you in public. In fact, they had stopped weighing you at all.

The positive thing about attending hospital was that I had some routine and structure, and at least each appointment followed the same pattern. I had nice ordered maternity notes which plotted my weight gain and tummy growth. They showed the results of my urine tests (powder and all) and my blood pressure, which was always consistent. It was orderly, routine based and made me feel secure. In my first three pregnancies I had the same consultant and I saw either him or his junior colleague. This consistency was reassuring and comforting even though the consultant's arrival in the clinic was like something from a *Carry On* film. He would stride in and sweep open the cubicle curtain. Not good news for you if you happened to be having your stomach palpated by a midwife at the time. By the end of my first pregnancy I think most of the hospital staff had seen my glorious stretch marks.

I have to admit, I didn't feel particularly prepared during this pregnancy. I was trying to cope with going from a vulnerable wild child who was usually out drinking and dancing four nights a week to a picture perfect wife and mother. I did what I had done throughout my life. I played a part. Having got through the first trimester – not exactly sailing through, more like limping – I approached the second trimester with some optimism.

The second trimester is pretty much like the first but a bit more magnified and at least you are getting closer to the end goal. The good news is that apparently during this trimester the morning sickness subsides. However, there is a get-out clause to that. For some women it stops and for others it can continue. I was one of the unlucky ones. I got to have morning sickness all day, every day, well into the second trimester. Even though the morning sickness may still be present, the positive thing about the second trimester is that during it you will get to week 20. If you work on the medical model, which loves numbers, week 20 is hailed as the halfway point. Kind of…

Pregnancy can last 38–42 weeks. For those of us on the autism spectrum, who are often rigid in thought and very literal, this can be difficult to take on board. My 'due date' changed twice in my first pregnancy. According to the date of my last menstrual period (LMP), my baby was due on 31 March. I went for a dating scan and they placed my due date at 7 March. My son was eventually born on 9 March. Interestingly, all of my first five children were due on 31 March but *none* of them were born then. Highly inconsiderate! I often wonder if there are any other people out there like me who have had a lot of children who were all due on the same date. Maybe I could take part in some kind of study!

HELPFUL HINTS

If you find that your due date is changing and this causes you anxiety, discuss it with your medical professional. Don't go home and worry about it and say nothing like I did. All that does is increase your anxiety. Even better, have an appointed advocate with you who can verbalise your concerns on your behalf.

The second trimester is also the time when antenatal classes are recommended. I attended one class during my first pregnancy and all I can remember is the midwife pushing a doll through a model of a pelvis. I didn't find it very helpful. I attended this class with my then husband but I felt uncomfortable and I also felt out of place because I was a lot younger than many of the other women there. I remember watching them and wondering what it would be like when I had grown up and was a 'real' woman. This feeling of being a little girl has been a constant throughout my life and I have found from working with other girls on the spectrum that very often there is this immaturity and naïvety. So I often sat in the antenatal ward thinking that maybe when I was a mother I would feel like a grown-up. I watched other women and wished I was them. This is something I still do now... I have never been happy with who I am.

The body changes continued but as the weeks progressed I began to notice the beginnings of a little bump. Feelings toward this change will be different for all women but I was extremely excited. The more inconvenient symptoms (mainly the nausea) became tolerable as I began to look pregnant. I could see the changes happening to my body, the fact that there was a little person growing inside me became more real. However, as I approached the final countdown (also known as the third trimester!), I began to feel the extra weight much more. During pregnancy you only need to increase your calorie intake in the final trimester, by around 200 calories per day.[3] But I had nearly doubled my body weight, going from six and a half stone to twelve stone, so I guess it was no wonder really. I had taken eating for two quite literally.

During those last three months of pregnancy I began to resemble a grumpy hippo. I had become used to not seeing my feet and I had aches in places I didn't know I had. My visits to the hospital became more frequent and my sensory challenges became more noticeable. Obviously, I hadn't been diagnosed with Asperger syndrome at this point so I didn't know I was experiencing sensory sensitivity. In fact, I also experienced regular meltdowns. I didn't realise that these were meltdowns – I assumed I was just crazy.

---

3   This is only a guideline as everyone is a different shape and size. For more information please see www.babycentre.co.uk.

What is a meltdown? A meltdown is where a person temporarily loses control due to emotional overload, which is usually a response to environmental factors. It may look as though the individual loses control over one thing. This is not the case. Imagine a bottle of fizzy drink. The bottle gets lots of shakes during the day and when it is eventually opened what happens? It explodes everywhere. This is how a meltdown works. There will have been a number of irritations that may have spanned over a day, a week or longer. Finally, the individual reaches breaking point and the meltdown will occur. To people who are unaware of meltdowns they can look like temper tantrums. In children there is often angry and sometimes violent behaviour such as hitting or kicking. In adults this can still be the case. However, the angry behaviour may take place at home or in private if the person with autism has developed the understanding that this behaviour is not socially acceptable in public. It may also turn inward and the adult on the spectrum may internalise those feelings and become disconnected and depressed. This may also lead to self-harming behaviours.

My meltdowns were frequent when I was pregnant for the first time. I think this was due to the huge amount of change I had undergone and was still experiencing. I also think a lot of my meltdowns were linked to changes in my hormones. I think there is much more research to be done on the impact of hormonal changes on people with autism. On the few occasions that my close family saw me in meltdown they would become alarmed and ask what was wrong. The thing to remember is that in the middle of a meltdown and for a period after, the ability to verbalise and rationalise is not there. It has left the building. Another thing to remember with meltdowns is that there is no single cause and no 'one size fits all'. Meltdowns can occur at different times and different frequencies. There may be a hormonal link just as there is with puberty, meaning that meltdowns can be more frequent during pregnancy.

HELPFUL HINTS

Have regular breaks from sensory stimuli. High levels of sensory sensitivity can contribute to meltdowns so try to give yourself frequent 'time outs'. I found that bouncing on my labour ball really calmed me down. Getting away from people and being outside also helped. There were many times during my last pregnancy when I was aware of the impact my sensory sensitivities were having on me and therefore I would walk out of the house into the front or back garden. I just needed to breathe and ground myself.

Still on the subject of sensory needs, it was during this stage in my pregnancy that I developed a rubber obsession. The smell and taste of rubber was something I craved. I chewed elastic bands and sniffed rubber hot water bottles. I regularly visited the trainer section in shoe shops so that I could have a really big sniff of the rubber trainers. I would like to say that this fetish disappeared after I gave birth, but it didn't and I still have it now!

The final trimester was the time when I felt the most tired and ungainly. I have difficulties with proprioception (knowing where my body is in space), and with my centre of gravity changed by the growing bump I became much more clumsy than usual. I was also more out of breath. I felt growing excitement that this new person whom I had been nurturing would soon be here. I didn't know if I was having a boy or girl and I spent lots of time lost in daydreams wondering what this baby would look like. On the flip side I had the unknown experience of labour to get through first. And it is unknown. Every labour is different – I should know, I've done it six times – and none of my labours was the same. I read books that described labour as 'just like period pain but more intense'. That's open to interpretation. Some women find period pain horrendous and others don't. It is difficult to quantify an individual's expectation of pain and then describe it. People have different pain thresholds and this applies to period pain as well as any other kind of pain.

In my third trimester I noticed stretch marks. Actually, I didn't notice them because they were underneath my bump. I felt quite smug and happy that I had avoided them. Then one day when I was attending the antenatal clinic the midwife said, 'Ooh…you've got some lovely stretch marks under there.' That's what you get for being smug. I hadn't even been able to rub any cream on them because I was oblivious to their existence. Nowadays, I no longer worry about how my stretch marks look; I think of them as a map of my children's journeys here.

Of course there are the other unpleasant physical changes, such as haemorrhoids (or piles, as they are commonly known). I wasn't sure whether I could face writing about them… telling everyone who reads this book that I have 24-year-old piles. Then I decided that they are too significant (literally) to ignore. Haemorrhoids are swellings that develop inside and around the anus (back passage). There is a network of small veins that become engorged with blood and swell. This is common in pregnancy due to increased pressure weighing down on the pelvic blood vessels. When I was diagnosed with them I was told that they clear up after pregnancy. Mine haven't, hence them being 24 years old. I'm not sure if this is because I had so many children close together or whether any woman who has developed them in pregnancy finds that they never clear up. I also don't know if some women are more prone to developing them than others. Discussing piles is not a conversation starter (even I know that), which is why I can't quite believe that I have disclosed them in this book!

Towards the end of my pregnancy I encountered heartburn. In this first pregnancy I used to take three 5ml spoonfuls of antacid remedy three times daily, as prescribed. By my final pregnancy I just kept a bottle by the bed and swigged from it regularly. Heartburn shouldn't even be called 'heartburn'; it should be called 'throat burn' because that's where I found most of the pain was.

Just when you think there is nothing new that pregnancy can throw at you, there are Braxton Hicks contractions. These contractions feel like the real thing except they stop. If they don't stop, then you're probably in labour. Of course, if you are hypersensitive to pain, these 'pretend contractions' can feel like the real thing. The usual advice is to time them. Here we go back to numbers again. Timing contractions comes with its own set of problems. When you're in a highly anxious state with your first baby and you're wondering if you are in fact in labour (not to mention it's the middle of the night and you're standing on the stairs in your nightie, wondering whether you should get dressed), remembering how to do the timing is slightly difficult. My problems with maths resurfaced. I could never remember whether or not you were supposed to time from the start of the contraction to the end, then time the interval between contractions, in which case I would forget how long the contraction lasted because I was too busy timing the break in between. Fortunately, my labours weren't that straightforward, so my inability to understand how to time contractions was only a problem during the many false alarms I encountered for about four weeks before my due date.

HELPFUL HINTS

Don't get too hung up on timing contractions. If it really is labour, you will be in no doubt about it and the contractions will just keep coming.

In the final trimester it's time to pack your hospital bag. In my first pregnancy I packed it very early on but in subsequent pregnancies I wasn't quite so enthusiastic. At the back of this book you will find a checklist for your maternity bag if you are a mum on the spectrum. I used the checklist provided for neurotypical mums prior to my diagnosis but packed a few autism-specific items when I had my final baby post-diagnosis.

There is nothing more amazing than seeing your baby for the first time. I hold a snapshot in my heart and mind of every one of my children's faces as I saw them for the first time. As someone who never wanted children I wonder what would have become of me if I had never had them. I fell in love with them before they were born but as our eyes locked for the first time I fell even harder. This feeling must be why women have more than one child. After every birth I was adamant that I was never going through that again… Famous last words!

I have extremely high levels of anxiety. I think that people with autism should be given a diagnosis of anxiety disorder at the same time as their diagnosis of autism. The majority of young people that I have worked with would say that their biggest disabler is their anxiety. I also consider myself to have a relatively high pain threshold. Unfortunately, the anxiety affects this and it is only after having six children that I have come to realise that in my labours which came before I was diagnosed with Asperger syndrome, I panicked. All of my children were born in hospital and, as I've already said, I don't like hospitals. However, 24 years ago, when I had my first child, hospital was where you gave birth. Birth had become quite medicalised and labour wards were not really geared up for more natural births – everything was very clinical, and there was no sign of a beanbag or aromatherapy oils in the hospital I attended. I had no idea that I had other birth options. The general consensus of society was that only 'alternative hippy people' had a natural birth. Since completing my doula training, I have realised that it is the medical interventions in childbirth that are the alternative. Birth is natural. Women have been doing it forever. Of course, there is a place for the medical model but that should be in the event of an emergency situation and it really shouldn't be considered the norm.

Having my first child in hospital set a pattern for the rest of my births. My first husband was also of the mindset that if he got me into hospital they would intervene, get it over quickly and he could go out and wet the baby's head. The routine was set so it never occurred to me to have a baby anywhere but in hospital. With hindsight, an awareness of myself and my own needs, as well as knowledge about other options may have encouraged me to have stayed at home much longer for the early stages of my labours and maybe even the births. If that had happened, it is possible that I wouldn't have found labour and birth so intervention heavy and traumatic.

HELPFUL HINTS

Do your research on where to have your baby. In most countries hospitals tend to offer an 'intervention-heavy' type of delivery. Birthing centres offer a more natural and holistic experience of giving birth.

Because I don't like hospitals, I began to experience sensory overload as soon as I entered the car park. The large buildings, hoards of people, cars, ambulances and medical staff overwhelmed me. Also, I have a tendency to overthink and so I imagined the life stories being played out in each ward: new lives coming into the world in maternity; people breathing their last breaths in other wards. I was overcome with emotion as I imagined the different scenarios. Sometimes it's very hard living inside my head.

With my first son I was blissfully oblivious as to what lay ahead. As I approached my due date I experienced lots of Braxton Hicks contractions, which I thought were rather painful so must be the real thing. Then they stopped. On a Wednesday evening two days before my due date I was in the midst of these practice contractions when my husband decided that enough was enough and we were heading off to the labour ward. Upon arrival I was assaulted by the sounds and smells and my legs started to walk the other way. Too late... I was admitted, placed in a room and given an internal examination. I was 'only' 2cm dilated. What an anti-climax. I felt sure that the baby was almost out. The staff decided to keep me in for observation so I spent the night on the antenatal ward listening to women screaming and groaning. It was horrendous. I was struggling to cope with being on a ward with other people. I had never been in hospital before and the reality of sharing a space with five other women was horrendous and alien to me. This was not a good start.

The next day I was examined – again, still 2cm. The decision was made to place me on a drip to begin the induction process. But first I had to have an enema. This was not something I was expecting and I was never given one again with any subsequent pregnancies. However, at that time it was standard practice. By now I was regretting having come to hospital and was considering whether it was too late to change my mind about having this baby. Unfortunately, it was too late. One way in, one way out, as a midwife put it. I was placed on the drip, which didn't have much of an effect, so I was taken off the drip and told to have a bath. This was one of their better ideas. I found the warm water very helpful and calming. To this day there is a certain scent from a bubble bath that takes me back to that day in the bath in the hospital.

As the evening progressed there was a very slow dilation (opening of the cervix) taking place but it was accompanied by a lot of pain. I was offered no pain relief until the early hours of Friday morning. I was given gas and air (although this is not readily offered in all countries). It was like being drunk, only it happened faster. This took a lot of the edge off the sensory overload and pain (which incidentally didn't feel like any period pain I had ever experienced). I found out later on in labour that my baby was in the wrong position – his back was against my back so that was why my labour was so painful and slow. Although the gas and air had helped with the pain, progress of the labour was still very slow and my baby was becoming distressed (pretty much like his mother).

A doctor was called for and he appeared gowned up brandishing forceps. By this point the gas and air was no longer helping and I was in full panic mode. Nobody explained what was happening and I felt completely out of control. I know now that it didn't have to be like that. I had been in hospital too long, which had heightened my anxiety, I had experienced too much clinical intervention and, most importantly, I had never met the midwives and medical staff who were taking care of me. So there I was with the doctor examining me when he suddenly told me to immediately stop pushing. I was only 8cm dilated and had developed a 'lip' on my cervix, which meant that my baby couldn't get past it. Lots of hushed conversation was taking place and in the end they decided to give me an epidural and wait for the lip to go down. So everything changed from the expectation that I would see my baby very soon to the fact that now I had to try to get some sleep and would be reassessed in the morning. I was devastated. I just wanted it to be over. To me it felt barbaric. I couldn't believe that you could be left in that kind of condition.

After a dreadfully uncomfortable night a different doctor appeared to examine me. At long last I was fully dilated and ready to push. To assist my birth they decided to use a ventouse (a bit like the suction from a vacuum cleaner) to help delivery. An epidural has the benefit of taking away pain but it also means that you cannot feel your contractions and therefore don't have a natural urge to push. At 9.50am my son came screaming into the world to an audience of staff. I had been in labour for 37 hours and some staff had stayed beyond their shift just to see him born. Had I known how popular my delivery was going to be I would have sold tickets! As soon as he was born the 15 or so people in the room crowded around him while I was left with the doctor as I delivered the placenta. Then he told me how I had torn quite badly so he needed to repair me. As everyone cooed over my beautiful boy I was in utter shock and began to shake. I thought I was dying. Nobody appeared to notice my distress as they were still cooing over the little prince who had taken so long to appear. This was not how it was supposed to be. It wasn't like this in any films or television programmes I had ever seen. I felt like a survivor of the apocalypse. But when they placed him in my arms and he looked at me with the biggest, bluest eyes as if he knew me better than I knew myself, I realised that all the pain had been worth it.

Following my son's birth I was left in the delivery room with him because there were no beds available on the ward. I sat there gazing at him and willing him not to wake up because if he woke up, I would have to pick him up and feed him and I didn't know how to do that. Inevitably he woke up and demonstrated the phenomenal pair of lungs he had. There is something primal in that when your baby cries all of your senses are telling you to comfort them to stop the crying. I pressed the buzzer to call for the midwife, my panic increasing with each of my son's screams.

Eventually a midwife came bustling in and picked him up. She handed him to me and asked if I knew how to latch him on. I wasn't sure what she meant so I said 'yes.' She asked me to show her. As he was nuzzling around I assumed she expected me to feed him. I shakily undid my nightdress and hoped that he knew what to do. He became more distressed and started to shake his head back and forth. He was getting redder and hotter and so was I. Realising that I obviously didn't have a clue, the midwife grabbed my breast and my son's head and put them together. Within minutes he was quiet and suckling away. The midwife bustled off, probably thinking how incompetent I was as she went to look after a 'proper' mother. After a couple of seconds my son pulled away from my breast and started screaming again. He looked furious and I felt useless. My eyes began to water and I wondered how I was ever going to cope if I couldn't even feed my own child.

After a while I was moved to a room in the postnatal ward with five other women and their babies. My expectation had been that all babies would be whisked off to a nursery and I would be resting serenely in my own room. I had obviously watched too many films as this was not the case! It was horrendous. I felt sick with anxiety. I wanted to keep the screens closed around my bed but the midwives kept opening them and I didn't want to ask for them to be shut because I was very conscious of the fact that the other mothers in the ward all had their screens open and were all discussing their birth stories. They didn't speak to me other than to say 'hello', and I wondered what it was about me that they didn't like. Why couldn't I have an easy conversation with them like they all seemed to be having with each other? Again, there was this feeling of still being a little girl watching the grown-ups. I watched how they seemed to effortlessly know how to interact with each other and it just made me feel more like a failure.

I had experienced such a difficult birth that I had to spend a couple of days sitting on an inflatable cushion because of the pain from my stitches. I was still having problems with breastfeeding my baby and I was told that he could sense my anxiety, which is why he was struggling to feed (my fault again). Then I was told he needed to have formula because he was looking a little orange. This was a sign of jaundice, which is common in newborns and more likely in completely breastfed babies. So the suggestion to top up with a bottle of formula seemed a sensible one and not a suggestion that I felt I should question. It was one that I came to regret. On day five I was discharged and so was my son even though he was still a little more orange than I felt he should be. We took him home and that's when reality sank in. I couldn't eat a meal or go to the bathroom without my son, who although he appeared to be fast asleep, would immediately wake up and shriek as though he was being tortured. I was exhausted and possibly delirious from lack of sleep.

The community midwife came in daily to check on my stitches and my son. The good news was that I was healing ok – possibly due to the fact that I was permanently attached to a rubber ring and a bag of frozen peas. The bad news was that my little man's jaundice was not improving, and following a blood test I was given the news that he had to return to hospital to receive treatment. To me this was a sign that I was an incompetent mother. I didn't understand that this happens to lots of newborn babies and is treatable in the majority of cases. I believed that this was my fault. So I headed back to the hospital that we had so recently left and handed my baby over for phototherapy light treatment. This entailed him being placed in an incubator under lights with an eye mask on. He looked so small and vulnerable that I was convinced something was dreadfully wrong with him.

I decided to stay overnight in the parents' room so that I could continue to breastfeed him. I went to sleep and woke up some time later with painful, leaking breasts and a feeling of panic. Why hadn't the nurses come to fetch me to feed my baby? I jumped out of bed and raced to the nurses' station, convinced that something had happened to my son. The nurse reassured me that he was fine and asleep. I asked why I hadn't been woken to feed him and was told that I had appeared to be in such a deep sleep they hadn't wanted to wake me so they gave him a bottle. I explained that my breasts were painful and they suggested that I use their breast pump, humorously called 'Daisy', to express my milk. This sounded like a plan so off I went to use it with a sterile bottle tucked into my dressing gown pocket. A nurse came with me to show me where it was and what to do. As we sat down and the pump began to work hardly anything came out. We tried for a while on both breasts and by the end there wasn't even a teaspoonful. I was so upset. It was only many years later, after what I considered to be failed attempts at breastfeeding all of my children, that I found out what the problem actually was.

The introduction of formula sounded the death knell for my attempt at breastfeeding my first child. Although I persevered with breastfeeding, it was hard once I had got used to seeing how much milk he took from a bottle. I became quite obsessed with making sure he had enough fluids when he came home from hospital. I was so worried that he would develop jaundice again and have to go back to hospital. I was still unable to successfully express my own milk even though I had bought my own pump. It became more satisfying to be able to see how much milk he had taken from a bottle. Of course, 24 years ago things were different to how they are now when it came to looking after a baby. Back then it was feed every four hours and put baby down to sleep on his front! Wake him up and start all over again. This style suited me as it was structured and routine based. I wrote down when he had fed and how much, and when he needed feeding again. I got satisfaction from making up his formula and counting scoops to fluid ounces. My son was a good baby. He seemed to adapt to this routine as well.

All in all, things were fine…except for the fact that I felt strange. I felt disconnected from my life and very isolated. My parents worked, my husband worked and I didn't have any friends to speak of. I carried out day-to-day tasks but I felt empty. I got upset quickly and became emotional over the smallest of things. Finally, I decided to see the doctor. I went and told him how I felt and he immediately diagnosed postnatal depression. He prescribed me antidepressants and told me that he would refer me for counselling. This was a taboo subject for me to discuss with my husband. He viewed depression and any kind of mental health issues as a weakness and a flaw in one's character. I think that once he knew this, instead of showing understanding, he stored it away and used it as a stick to beat me with. I was referred to a community psychiatric nurse (CPN) who came and visited me at home.

He encouraged me to take my medication but I didn't. I was massively pills phobic and instead I flushed them down the toilet. However, I did begin to respond to the therapy with him. We did relaxation and talking therapy and it was the first time that anyone had really listened to me and validated my feelings.

I decided that I wanted to return to work and secured a job as an office assistant, starting work when my son was six months old. My mum offered to give up work to look after him and this made me feel happier as she was the only person that I trusted with him. Once at work I felt better and my sessions with the CPN finished as I was working full time. A few months later I developed an eye condition and became quite ill. I was given steroids to treat it and was suffering with the side effects of those as well as working full time and being a mum. I enjoyed my job and had no plans to have another baby after my first experience. However, when my first son was 18 months old I became pregnant again.

Chapter 4

MATTHEW

At the start of my second pregnancy I was struggling with a severe eye condition. I was being medicated with a large dose of steroids, which came complete with unpleasant side-effects. I had an active toddler and I was working full time. The last thing I had been considering was another baby. I went to my GP because I felt unwell. During the course of treatment for my eye condition I had endured numerous tests including a magnetic resonance imaging (MRI) scan to rule out a brain tumour. I told the doctor my symptoms, which I was concerned could be a side-effect of my eye problem or the medication I was taking to treat it. He looked at me and said, 'It sounds like you're pregnant.' In that instant pregnancy was a relief as I had thought I was suffering from something more sinister. I was offered a pregnancy test, which was positive, and the arrival of baby No. 2 was scheduled for the same date as baby No. 1 had been two years earlier. Then the shock set in. I was terrified. I was very ill and taking strong medication for that illness, and I worked full time. Money was tight as we had a mortgage to pay and I had no idea how we would manage.

When I told the consultant who was taking care of my eye condition that I was pregnant, he delivered a devastating blow. He told me that I would need to consider a termination of the pregnancy or run the risk of permanently losing my sight. He had to take me off steroids due to the pregnancy and he didn't know how my eye condition would respond. I was in a terrible situation. Termination had never been an option for me. I would never judge any other woman for what they chose to do but I knew that it was something I couldn't do. I decided that whatever happened I was going to continue with the pregnancy. The first trimester was filled with anxiety as I was weaned rapidly off steroids and I spent many sleepless nights as I wondered what would happen to my sight. I was also unsure what to do about my job. I loved my work and was good at it, and my employer offered a good childcare package. My mum didn't feel able to cope with two young children so the only other option was nursery provision. My husband was keen for me to stay at home with the children, and after thinking long and hard about it I decided that this was the best option.

Throughout this pregnancy I kept myself busy with work as well as keeping a check on my health. Interestingly, my eye condition seemed to improve and it was a fantastic day when I was finally discharged from the eye hospital. My ophthalmic consultant was pleased and surprised as he had thought that the pregnancy would be detrimental to the eye condition. I had decided to work as long as I possibly could and I finally finished work when I was 37 weeks pregnant. On my last day at work my employer told me that he had asked his church members to pray for me and my baby and my eyesight. I was immensely touched by this and it made me think of the power of prayer and how much more there was in the universe than we can possibly know about. It tapped into my spiritual nature, which I still had a strong connection with. Amazingly, considering how the pregnancy had started off, I felt well throughout it.

I worked until 37 weeks with no problems at my antenatal visits. At 39 weeks I attended a funeral and felt awful throughout the proceedings. I thought nothing of it as I assumed I was probably very emotional, especially since I was only one week away from having my baby. Following the funeral I returned to the wake and drank copious amounts of tea with lots of sugar. Many people at the wake commented on my thirst for tea and suggested that maybe I would have the baby very soon. I didn't really take them seriously as my first son had been later than my due date and I just assumed that my second would be the same. The funeral was an hour and a half away from home and as my husband drove us home I was having regular contractions. When we arrived I fell into bed exhausted. I was daring my body really. If it was labour then I wouldn't sleep through it – I was certain of that.

I awoke the next morning and could hardly lift my head off the pillow. My head was pounding and I had flashing lights when I opened my eyes. I instantly felt that something was very wrong and so I telephoned the GP. He paid a home visit, took one look at me and said I needed to go straight to hospital. My hands, feet and face were swollen and my blood pressure was high. I had developed pre-eclampsia. Strangely enough, I wasn't worried. In fact, I was borderline euphoric. I have heard from other women that pre-eclampsia can make you feel very out of character. The doctor wanted to call an ambulance but I really didn't want to do that and I was quite belligerent as I told him that I was not travelling in an ambulance, I would get a lift. My parents came and took me in as my husband was not in the area.

When I got to hospital I was already 3cm dilated. Induction and enema not required. After a ten hour labour my second son was born. This time I only had gas and air for pain relief and my boy rushed into the world impatiently. He still tackles life in pretty much the same way. I experienced the same social anxiety the minute I was taken to the postnatal ward and I endured my time there again with gritted determination and open screens.

I was sent home two days later and introduced my sons to each other. While my first son had been such a placid baby, my second son was quite different. He was very vocal. I had read all about how to make the best start at breastfeeding and I felt certain that this time I would succeed. I began breastfeeding him and this time I knew what 'latched on' meant – he was great at latching on and feeding. He had his initial loss of weight (like all babies do) but everything seemed to be going ok. He was breastfeeding constantly and I was determined to keep going.

Nevertheless, I began to worry because I couldn't tell exactly how much milk he was taking. I felt drawn to giving him formula so that I could see the actual amount. I resisted the temptation though as I had seen the 'Breast is Best' posters plastered around the hospital. When he was next weighed, the midwife was concerned because he hadn't gained any weight. She suggested I top him up with formula. I was completely disheartened. She suggested that the problem could be that he was a big baby (I now know that his size wouldn't have made any difference). Once he started to take formula, he became more settled, and again I was left feeling that there was something wrong with me because of my inability to feed my babies. On the plus side, I was back to the comforting routine of measuring formula scoops and being able to see how much milk he had taken at each feed.

As the days turned to months and I developed a routine with the boys, I found myself very lonely again. I had been warned by medical staff that I was more likely to get postnatal depression because I had suffered with it before. I didn't feel depressed though; I just felt disconnected again. I was excellent at taking care of my children. I had a routine that was well established but I struggled to play with them. I bought them lots of toys – probably too many – but I found playing imaginatively with them really hard. Of course, now I know that this is part of my autism – it makes perfect sense, but at the time I just didn't understand myself. I had all the old feelings of being frustrated with myself come flooding back. I felt scared on a daily basis but I didn't know what I was scared of. I began to long for another baby. I began to crave the familiarity of the routine of pregnancy checks and hospital visits. I missed the routine of the hospital and I felt the desire to bury myself in my special interest again. I loved thinking about what my baby would look like and be like, and I also felt that the more children I had, the less lonely I would feel. Make way for baby No. 3.

Chapter 5

DANIEL

With baby No. 3 I knew the day my period was due that I was pregnant. Again, it was a feeling. By this time I was a stay-at-home mum mainly because this was what my husband wanted but also because in my own mind I couldn't trust anyone else, other than my mum, to look after my children. With the benefit of hindsight I think having the children was also my protection from the world of socialising. I didn't recognise it then as I didn't have a diagnosis but I see it now. I had lost a lot of confidence since leaving work and having my second child. If I was a mother, I really didn't have to go out and interact with other people other than on a superficial level in the shops etc. My eldest son was at part-time nursery so it seemed like a good idea to be at home with my 18-month-old and a new baby. With this pregnancy I had the same nausea in the first trimester, and the exhaustion this time was overwhelming. I caught every cold and virus going round and I felt utterly miserable and isolated.

By now the cracks were beginning to show in my marriage and my husband had a job which required him to socialise regularly with clients. There were many nights he came home hours after he said he would, usually when the children were in bed. I felt as though my whole life was like *Groundhog Day* and I felt isolated and cut off. The light at the end of this tunnel was my third child and, of course, my two wonderful sons.

I developed a craving for coconut macaroons and ate them by the packet. My rubber craving reared its head again and I spent many happy hours sniffing hot water bottles. I had my routine of taking my eldest son to nursery and then wandering round the shops with my youngest son. I would pop into the shop where my mum worked or visit my grandma. I enjoyed this daily routine as it was repetitive, predictable and safe. I only went to places I was familiar with and spent time with people that I knew well.

My world was becoming very small and insular. I was also experiencing tremendous stress at having to play the role of a trophy wife. My husband's job required lots of socialising and sometimes partners were required to attend. I found these events dreadful. The anxiety would begin days beforehand. I would make up excuses not to attend, because I was unable to tell him that I just didn't like being around people I didn't know. He wouldn't have understood anyway and it would have been another reason for him to be critical of me.

Before social occasions (the ones I hadn't managed to get out of), I would change outfits numerous times because I didn't think I looked 'right'. I would re-apply make-up over and over again because it didn't look perfect. I was exhausted before we even got there. Then the anxiety would peak. I felt awkward having to speak to people and I just didn't know what to say. I wasn't interested in them as I didn't know them, so why would I want to talk to them? I found these occasions boring and tiring. I struggled to understand people's humour and I would feel as though they were making fun of me. It was a superficial world where everyone discussed how much money they had and the wives all eyed each other to see who was wearing what. Initially I had managed to perform my way through these occasions but as time went on I began to dread them more and more. I found going out and interacting with people I hardly knew very difficult. There was no discussing this with my husband as he just accused me of being awkward. All of this began to make life complicated. I couldn't understand why I despised these events so much. Everyone else appeared to enjoy them but I didn't. When I got home at the end of the evening my face would ache from smiling and I would feel exhausted and emotional. At least being pregnant again gave me an excuse to avoid these arduous events.

On top of all this, I couldn't get to toddler groups as much as I might have liked, and I often felt guilty about this. But then there wasn't much at that time in my life that I didn't feel guilty about. I tried to compensate for this by purchasing lots of toys for my children. My house rapidly began to resemble a toy superstore. There was a storm building up with the amount of pressure I was under and it was only a matter of time before things came to a head.

During this pregnancy I noticed that times were changing at the hospital and there was a birthing pool available for those mothers who wanted a more 'alternative' labour. I knew how much I loved being in the water and how comforting I found it, so the birthing pool appealed to me. Apart from feeling rundown, this pregnancy was fairly uneventful. I took this to be a good sign. I was sure that this must mean that labour and birth would be even more straightforward than last time. As my second labour had been ten hours and usually subsequent labours are shorter, I was banking on about five hours for this one. Again, my due date came and went. I spent a lot of time examining my underwear for a plug of mucus and waking up hoping to feel a pool of water from the amniotic fluid sac bursting. None of this happened. The fifth day after my due date found me miserable and having the odd weak contraction. This was enough to trigger my husband into taking me into hospital to get it all over and done with.

It was a beautiful Easter Sunday but the drawback was there was only a skeleton staff on the labour ward as it was a holiday period. I went into hospital with fairly weak, irregular contractions but the water pool was available so I got in. The water was immensely helpful and soothing. I was quite happy to float about in there as the contractions began to intensify.

After a few hours of what was deemed slow progress, the midwife suggested that she rupture my waters to 'get things moving'. I was hesitant as I had heard that once this was done the pain and pace of labour would increase. My husband was all for it as he had finished reading his newspaper and wanted to get it over and done with so he could go home to sleep. I bowed to his persuasion and pressure and agreed that my waters could be broken. This was a bad move. Within an hour of this being done the pain I was experiencing was excruciating. (This was mainly because the baby's head had been resting quite happily on the amniotic sac prior to the sac being suddenly burst, but then abruptly hit the pelvic bone without any prior warning.) The pain was so intense I didn't know what to do with myself. I no longer felt calmed by the water and I was beginning to become even more anxious and panicky. I stood up in the pool but that felt uncomfortable, so I sat down again and that was worse. Then I noticed bright red blood and suddenly the atmosphere changed in the room.

There was a tangible sense of panic and more and more people started arriving. I was told to get onto the bed to be examined but that hurt and I began to shut down mentally. I remember being in a haze of almost semi-consciousness. I had selected my birth playlist, which had been helpful during the calm time spent in the birthing pool. Now I could vaguely hear the Blur song 'Girls and Boys' but it seemed a long way off. I could also hear snippets of conversation – people were talking about how the baby was becoming distressed and discussing what my blood group was because I needed a transfusion. Then a midwife with an air of authority around her came in, declaring that the baby needed to come out. She spoke to me in a soothing but direct tone with a lilting Irish accent and I began to feel calmer. She explained that she was going to perform an episiotomy and get baby out as quickly as possible as he was tired and distressed and so was I. I began to refocus and listened to the instructions she gave. Hers was the only voice I tuned into as I began to push my baby out. Within a relatively short time and after a few hefty pushes, I heard my baby cry and he was whisked away to check he was well.

Again, I was in a state of shock. What had happened to my calm water birth? How had it all gone wrong so quickly? In my opinion, medical intervention had caused the problem. I hadn't followed my own instincts; instead I was coerced into doing something that was against my better judgement. This was another isolating experience and I felt as though I had let myself and my baby down.

HELPFUL HINTS

I cannot recommend enough the benefits of having an advocate with you during labour and birth. If a partner can't be this person, then consider someone else you trust. It is vital that your voice is heard, and for mums on the spectrum someone advocating for them is a necessity.

A week after leaving hospital I experienced a haemorrhage while out shopping with my son. I had to return to the hospital immediately and was told I needed to stay overnight. I declined and went home, promising to return the next morning to have an internal scan. I was sure that the scan would show that all was well so I returned to the hospital with only my baby son for company. The scan showed that I had some retained placenta. I was sent home and told to return later that day for a procedure to remove the placenta that would be carried out under general anaesthetic. This whole experience rocked me to the core. I had never had a general anaesthetic before and I didn't know what it would be like. I was 'nil by mouth' (not allowed to eat or drink before the operation) for the rest of the day, and as I sat in the lounge listening to my other boys and looking at my tiny newborn son I felt melancholic. I was certain that I wouldn't wake up from the general anaesthetic and my imagination drifted down a dark path. I went into hospital for the dilation and curettage (D and C), a brief surgical procedure that involved opening the cervix and then scraping the lining of the uterus...a procedure that I am sure is much better undertaken while asleep. I did wake up from the anaesthetic and I was discharged the next morning.

While I was in hospital my new baby was given formula, so again there was an interference with breastfeeding. I had been experiencing similar problems with breastfeeding as before, but this time I gave in earlier to the use of a bottle. Back to the familiar measuring of formula and knowing how much my baby had taken. I had resigned myself to the fact that I couldn't breastfeed. I kept telling midwives that I thought it was because my breasts were too small and seemed different to other women's that I had seen on television (and even my own mother's). I was told that I was being oversensitive and that I just had big babies who were ferociously hungry.

Around this time my vision of a happy family life had begun to disappear. My husband was indifferent to me and our children and spent more and more time out of the house. When my third son was about 12 months old, we moved house. Within three months my husband had moved out for the first time.

Chapter 6

CHARLOTTE

With my fourth pregnancy again I knew I was pregnant before my period was due. This time, though, my marriage was terminal. My husband had moved out for a week but then came back and it was then I became pregnant. He moved out again, this time for good, when I was four months pregnant. Due to the stress of the marriage split the first trimester of my fourth pregnancy passed in a haze. In one way, him leaving was devastating and it destroyed the picture I had in my head of the family life that my children would experience. On the other hand, it was a relief. I no longer had to walk around on eggshells wondering where he was, who he was with, and would I need to have the boys in bed before he came back. It also gave me some control, which I felt had been lacking in my life as a married woman. I was a shadow of my former self and had become compliant and downtrodden.

Being on my own with my boys was hard but it also gave me some autonomy, which my Aspie self had been craving. Physically and emotionally the pregnancy was difficult. I was trying to bring up three boys under the age of six on my own. At the same time I was trying to understand the behaviour of my husband and explain his absence to my children. Fortunately, I had my parents, who selflessly gave their time and support to myself and the boys. During this time the repetitive behaviours that I had experienced as a child resurfaced. I would check and re-check doors, and switch light switches on and off an even number of times. My primary concern was my boys. I wanted them to have everything they needed and more. As I was trying to keep life steady for them, I was neglecting myself. I wasn't eating properly and I certainly wasn't sleeping even though I was constantly exhausted. In the darkness of the night when the boys were asleep my mind would run riot with thoughts of the future and what would become of us.

When I was five months pregnant my mother was diagnosed with breast cancer. This was a horrendous time for us as a family. My children's father was totally unsupportive and absent and my wonderful parents were worrying about me but also going through their own life-changing situation. I felt completely alone. I made the hospital visits on my own, feeling as though I was in a fog most of the time. This is where an advocate or key support person would have been useful, not just for a person with autism but for any woman in this difficult situation.

Due to my excessive anxiety (and, as I now know, my being on the spectrum), I constantly overshared. I had no awareness of appropriate boundaries. I cried and talked and found it hard to control my emotions. I had many more meltdowns than usual but I was also trying to internalise a lot of these feelings as I didn't want my children to be taken into care. I was exhausted and overwhelmed. I would then feel ashamed at having become so emotional in front of people. This feeling of shame was exacerbated by the fact that my absent husband had constantly berated me with the fact that I was over-emotional and that was a bad thing. These days (after lots of counselling, including trauma therapy), I know that feeling emotions is absolutely fine. Feeling them so acutely is also fine and is in line with being a female on the spectrum. I overshared with checkout operators, school teachers and the milkman! I have now learned that you need to know when to stop telling people your intimate details. I send apologies to those poor checkout operators and especially to the milkman who also had to cope with my youngest son calling him daddy whenever he came to collect our milk coupons.

I have now learned that if anyone asks me how I am, I should use stock phrases, depending on who is asking. It's based on a circle of trust, which is something I use with the young people I work with. If the person asking how I am is someone I don't know very well, then I will answer, 'I'm fine thanks. How are you?' If it's a work colleague in my team, I might be a little more honest and say, 'I'm not too bad thanks. How are you?' If it's one of the few people who are in my inner circle, it's ok to tell them how I really feel. I have found that training myself to use this script has worked well for me. It's always a good idea to develop a bank of stock phrases and to avoid oversharing unless it's with someone in your circle of trust. I have also learned as I have become more socially aware that when neurotypical people ask you how you are, they don't usually want to hear the truth.

HELPFUL HINTS

Practise conversations and put in boundaries. Be aware that females on the spectrum overshare, and try to remember that less is best. Draw a circle of trust and consider what you will share and with who.

This was such an awful time in my life. Often after the children had gone to bed I would lie awake for long stretches in the night thinking about my past and my future. How had I ended up in such a mess? I was scared that I would die giving birth to this baby, and my children would have nobody. I would often go and sit in their rooms in the dark and just watch them sleep and pray that I would live through this birth and be there for them. I was also terrified of being a single parent forever. But I think the thing that shattered my world the most was that the family picture I had in my head had been taken away. Although my marriage had not been planned, I had decided at the start that I would do everything I could to make it work. I never wanted my children to experience a family breakdown and this was the thing that kept me awake long into the night. I felt that I had got everything wrong and I wanted to go back to the start and re-do my life. Black and white thinking at its best.

During this pregnancy, antenatal classes were not uppermost in my mind. I was just glad to have got through another day. I spent a lot of time in the hospital as I kept having a threatened early labour due to stress. It was during one of these admissions that I met a midwife who became very helpful to me through this dark time. She offered to give me some individual support sessions. Really these seemed to be more about offloading and counselling than breathing techniques. I was grateful because she was an independent person who was not emotionally involved in my life. Sadly, she relocated before I had my daughter so was unable to be present during my labour and birth. It was during these one-to-one sessions that the midwife suggested it would be a good idea for me to have a scan to find out the sex of the baby. The reasoning behind this was because I currently had three boys and I really wanted a daughter but everyone felt that the chances of me having another boy were quite high. As I had previously suffered with postnatal depression it was felt that if I was having a fourth boy it would be better for me to be aware so that I would be prepared for that – preparation for change or, at least, preparation for what was coming next.

I think that for many women on the spectrum, finding out the sex of their baby is important and should be supported. However, this was in the days when knowing the sex of your baby was not as common as it is now. I was so excited because, as much as I wanted a daughter, I knew that whatever the sex of this baby was we had been through so much together that I couldn't wait to meet him or her. It also meant I would know whether to buy boy's clothes or girl's clothes. I had my scan and was told the unbelievable news that I was having a girl. I was thrilled – this somehow made up for the fact that my marriage was over. I would have loved a son as well, of course, but to have a daughter was wonderful news. This news didn't encourage my husband to come back to our family but that was, and still is, his loss. This news made me even more impatient because I couldn't wait for my daughter to be born.

The due date for my daughter was again bizarrely 31 March. As I had such a difficult home situation and the start of April was Easter again (I was keenly aware of what had happened when I had my last baby at Easter), I asked the consultant if I could be booked in for an induction on 31 March. He wasn't very keen and said that he would prefer to wait until I was more overdue. I found his attitude quite frustrating because what I was asking for made sense to me. Fuelled by an eagerness to meet my first daughter and also being completely exhausted, I pressed for a date. I was given 5 April. This was not ideal as it was only two days after my son's birthday (something he hasn't forgiven me or his sister for 20 years later) but it was also Good Friday. Nevertheless, it was either then or the week after. My impatience won and I agreed to 5 April although I felt sure that she would come naturally before then. I was wrong and so I was admitted to the antenatal ward bright and early on Good Friday.

I was in a side room and on my own. This was a massive plus point as I had no sensory or social distractions to deal with. At about 10.00am I was given my first prostaglandin pessary to begin induction. I got up and walked around but nothing much was happening. I read my magazines and ate chocolate and felt generally well and relaxed. After about five hours I was examined internally and as there seemed to be very little progress I was given another pessary. Within a couple of hours I was contracting quite well.

I had hired a transcutaneous electrical nerve stimulation (TENS) machine for pain relief. A TENS machine is a small, portable battery-operated device which is worn on the body and attached to the skin by sticky pads. Small electrical pulses are transmitted to the body much the same as tiny electric shocks. I have to say that personally I didn't find the machine that helpful in managing my pain.

As the contractions became intense and more regular quite quickly, I was moved down to the delivery suite for some gas and air. I was taken into a room and examined internally again to check on my progress. The midwife informed me that I was 5cm dilated and therefore it would probably be a while before I would give birth. I felt rather disgruntled at that as I had thought I was ready to push. I had an overwhelming urge to have a pee so I got up to go to the bathroom. As I walked across the room I heard a pop and felt a surge of water down my legs. At long last, after three previous children, my waters had burst just like they did on the television! As that happened, I had a strong urge to push. The midwife came back and examined me, telling me that I probably wasn't ready to push as I had only just been 5cm dilated. As she examined me she exclaimed that I was actually fully dilated and ready to push. Within 20 minutes I had roared my gorgeous girl out and she came screaming loudly into the world like a mini tornado. I was exhilarated. That had been by far my best experience of birth. Even vomiting into the gas and air mask hadn't diminished the joy I felt after that birth.

HELPFUL HINTS

Follow your body's instincts. Remember it can give birth and it will give birth. If you're the kind of Aspie who is very sensory, take some visuals into the birthing room so you can focus on them.

Following this birth I was given a room on my own, which I had requested. This changed my postnatal experience in hospital tremendously. It eased my anxiety and reduced the sensory overload I had been used to experiencing. It also gave me time to bond with my daughter and come to terms with my life as a single parent. At last I had the chance to rest and regain some energy. Interestingly, I didn't suffer with depression after I had my daughter. I wonder how much of an impact such a good birth and postnatal experience had on my more positive mindset and lack of postnatal depression. There was a new future awaiting me. Not what I had planned maybe, but one that I felt was going to be ok. I had my little family and as far as I was concerned that was it. There would be no more children for me as I didn't think I would ever trust a man again. I also didn't want my children to have further upheaval in their lives and, if I'm honest, I quite like being the only adult in my home.

With my first daughter I was again determined to breastfeed. My health visitor had arranged for a carer from social services to come in to do household chores. In one way I appreciated this but in another I actually hated the thought of this woman coming into my house. I found it stressful and I didn't know what to ask her to do. My home was my refuge and I didn't like the feeling of a stranger entering it. She was contracted to come for three weeks, beginning upon my return home from hospital, but after a week I could no longer take the stress of waiting for her to come (she didn't stick to the same time every day) and then having her in my house. I decided that it wasn't working and I ended the contract. This would have been fine but being a lone parent with a new baby and three children under six was not easy. Even though I was more positive in my mindset, physically I was exhausted. I was still trying to breastfeed exclusively and my daughter was a natural. She had no problems latching on like the boys had, and I really enjoyed the whole experience.

HELPFUL HINTS

Some women on the spectrum may experience sensory issues with breastfeeding. If you do, then it's fine to bottle-feed. You have to do what's best for you, and if you're anxious and struggling with breastfeeding, then it won't be a happy experience for you or your baby.

All of my children experienced formula feeding and they are all healthy and fine. However, my difficulties with breastfeeding weren't sensory. Although the initial signs were all in favour of successful breastfeeding this time around, my daughter wasn't gaining any weight. My health visitor thought that maybe this was because I wasn't looking after myself very well as I wasn't eating much during the day because I was so exhausted. After a couple of weeks things weren't improving so yet again I found myself turning to formula to top up my daughter's feeds.

The old self-doubt returned along with the feelings of being a failure. This time, though, these feelings were accompanied by a feeling of anger and resentment at the circumstances that had led me to be in this position. I felt alone and exhausted, and I am convinced that my daughter saved my life. She was a happy, smiling baby, and every morning when she woke up and beamed at me, she gave me the strength to get through the day. I'm not ashamed to say that my thoughts had regularly turned to suicide since the breakdown of my marriage, but my children, especially my tiny daughter, gave me the will to live.

It was during this time that I began to experience quite intense and frequent migraines. I had never experienced them before and the first time the visual disturbances began I was holding my daughter and I was terrified that I was having a brain haemorrhage or a stroke. Ever since then, I have had these intense visual disturbances and headaches whenever I am experiencing high levels of anxiety, or at particular times of the month coinciding with hormonal changes in my body. Nevertheless, even though this was a fraught and difficult time, I found living on my own with my children quite a positive experience. I had my routine, which I gained comfort from, and there was no other adult telling me what to do or what not to do. I have realised over time that I am fine being on my own, and I find it difficult, especially as I am getting older, to live with another adult.

Chapter 7

OLIVIA

Three years later I had met my second husband and we were due to get married, when I found out that I was pregnant again. We had been trying for a baby so for the first time in my life I found myself actively waiting for the date of my period to see if I was pregnant, and when the test was positive we were both overjoyed. I hadn't expected to meet someone who would make me happy after my disastrous first marriage, so to meet someone and be about to get married to him was wonderful. I was back in 50s housewife mode with a house full of children. This time I was living with a man who appreciated it. The pregnancy was the icing on the cake. With this pregnancy I didn't have any symptoms like I had with my other children. I put this down to the fact that I had a different partner now, so maybe my body was reacting differently. Unfortunately, this wasn't the case.

I was working as a childminder at the time, so I put my lack of pregnancy symptoms partly down to the fact that I was just too busy and tired to notice them. I was desperate to tell my other children but I waited until I had passed the 12-week date when the risk of miscarriage is supposed to lessen. Being very literal I told them at 12 weeks and one day. The children were thrilled and excited at the prospect of a new sibling and discussed their preferences for a brother or a sister. With three boys in the house, a brother was overwhelmingly for the favourite! A week later I had a nightmare that was strange and unnerving and there was a high-pitched scream that I could hear in my sleep, but then I awoke and could still hear it. I got out of bed feeling confused and my body felt like lead. The high-pitched noise had stopped and I attributed it to the nightmare I had been in the midst of. I pushed it to the back of my mind and I got ready as quickly as I could because I was expecting the children that I cared for to be dropped off any time.

As the day went on I felt worse and thought that I was probably coming down with a virus. I completed the school run and as the last of the children in my care were collected my mind was on what to cook my own children for their supper. It was then that I felt a strange pop in my stomach and for some reason my mind went back to the high-pitched scream I had heard in my dream…the dream that had left me with an unsettled feeling all day. I went to the bathroom and realised that I was bleeding. Not a major bleed, no excruciating pain like miscarriages are portrayed in most drama series on the television. But I knew this was different for me. I had never had any spotting or bleeding of any kind during my previous pregnancies so I panicked.

I raced up to the doctor's and as the surgery was about to close the receptionist told me that she would have a word with the doctor on duty for emergencies. The doctor didn't even ask to see me. I heard her talking to the receptionist, telling her to send me home as most women have some spotting in their pregnancies. Instead of demanding to see someone because I knew this was different for me, I didn't. I went home and spent a sleepless night, willing the baby to hang in there. I think I had been labelled as highly anxious by my doctor and I wish now that I had demanded to see someone. If you are the kind of person who has massive anxiety, don't feel ashamed of it. Anxiety is not a weakness or a character flaw. If anything, people who suffer with anxiety and depression are the strongest of all characters because they keep on going.

The next morning I was still experiencing light bleeding so I bypassed the doctor's surgery and telephoned the Early Pregnancy Unit (EPU) at the hospital where I had given birth to my other children. I was given an appointment that afternoon. I spent the rest of the day lying down even though I knew from information on the Internet that if I was miscarrying at this stage of pregnancy there was nothing that could be done to stop it.

My partner and I went to the hospital and waited for a midwife to see us. We explained what had been happening and she tried her best to reassure us. We were sent for an ultrasound scan. It was then that we were told that the sac was empty. There was no heartbeat. Our baby was dead. We were told this in a very matter-of-fact tone by the radiographer. He then left to call another medical person to verify his findings. My partner and I were devastated. I was 13 weeks pregnant. As we left the hospital we walked past pregnant women on their way to their antenatal appointments and I knew that when I returned there in a few days it would be to have the remnants of my baby 'evacuated', which is the medical terminology used.

As it turned out, I returned to the hospital sooner than I thought because the next night I began to bleed heavily. My husband-to-be rushed me down to the emergency department and they decided to keep me in overnight and perform the evacuation procedure the next day. My fear of hospitals was at its highest peak. I spent the night in a lot of pain and was eventually given an injection of the drug pethidine. This didn't really help; in fact, it made me feel sick and caused me to feel anxious and panicky. This was my nightmare come true. My sons were away with their father and my daughter was with my parents. I was certain that I was going to die and would never see them again. My children didn't even know that I had lost the baby. I was taken to theatre the next morning, where I experienced my second general anaesthetic, and in the afternoon I was discharged with leaflets about miscarriage. I was angry, depressed and devastated. Physically, I felt like an empty shell. I really did feel as though I was empty inside.

The miscarriage affected me deeply. I had spent most of my life feeling like a failure at everything the rest of my peers seemed to succeed at effortlessly. I had hated school and dropped out of college. I had put myself in risky situations and become dependent on alcohol. I had married a man for all the wrong reasons and now had a broken marriage behind me. The one thing that I had been good at was having babies and being a mother. With the miscarriage I felt as if this was something else I had failed at. I can also recognise now that my special interest had been taken away. This was not in the plan and I hated my lack of control over the situation.

I felt everything so deeply – again, a part of being an Aspie – and I didn't think I would ever get over this loss. I didn't wash or get dressed for days. I sat in front of the television, not watching it, and every now and then my eyes would fill with tears and then spill over to run silently down my cheeks. I couldn't stop the tears from coming; I felt like my eyes were constantly leaking. Well-meaning family members kept telling me that everything would be ok and that it obviously wasn't meant to be. That was really not helpful and just made me feel as though I was overreacting, which of course I wasn't. We lost our baby on 24 May, and I felt sure 'it' would have been a boy. We planted a rose bush named 'Peace' in the garden to acknowledge his brief existence in our lives.

Based on this experience, my advice would be that if you have any worries and experience *any* bleeding during your pregnancy, then go with your instincts and seek medical advice. Don't be fobbed off as overanxious. Yes, it is true that many women experience light spotting during pregnancy, but I knew my body and I knew that the bleeding was not something I had ever experienced before. I know medical intervention wouldn't have stopped my miscarriage but it would have answered my questions sooner and validated my feelings. It would also have given me appropriate treatment earlier instead of the late-night rush into the emergency department, where I had to sit in a cubicle in the midst of drunken weekend revellers. Although I waited for the 12-week time before telling my children, I still lost my baby; and even if I had not told them, they would have known that something was very wrong because of the grief I was experiencing.

We considered postponing the wedding, which was due to take place two weeks after I lost the baby. In the end we decided we couldn't upset the children anymore because they were so excited about the wedding. I did feel as though I was just going through the motions of carrying out the final preparations. When I went to have my wedding dress fitting, the staff, who knew that I had been pregnant, were commenting on how I hadn't put much weight on and how well the dress fitted. I didn't try to correct them. I was shutting down and retreating into myself. The week leading up to the wedding brought dreadful weather conditions. These conditions mirrored my feelings. Although it was early June, there was lots of wind and rain, but on the morning of our wedding the sun was streaming through my bedroom window, forming a sunshine halo around my wedding dress. For the first time in weeks I felt positive about the future. The wedding was perfect. The boys were pages and my daughter looked like a little ball of net and lace as our bridesmaid. I couldn't have asked for anything better and I felt that after living in the dark for so long I was coming out into the light.

The one issue that still niggled away at me was the desire for a child with my second husband. However, I was terrified to go through pregnancy again and I worried that maybe I wouldn't be able to have a child with a man that I was actually in love with. I had taken to using the Internet to search for a cause for the miscarriage and I had convinced myself that I had miscarried because of a compatibility problem between myself and my husband. I began to obsess about this and was sure that we would never be able to have a child together. I need not have worried because a couple of weeks after our wedding I began to feel sick, tired and emotional. My breasts were tender and I was a constant visitor to the toilet. Yes, I was pregnant. Our little miracle was conceived on our wedding night.

With this pregnancy the first trimester symptoms were very strong. I made many visits to the doctor, who tried to reassure me that this was a good sign. However, I was still feeling nervous and I had this feeling of dread that something bad would happen again. I kept reliving the miscarriage over and over. I desperately tried to remember if there was anything I had done that could have been a trigger, so that I could try to avoid it this time. Now I know that miscarriage is one of those things that, unfortunately, is quite common in early pregnancy.

The health of this baby was foremost in my mind. Although I had been anxious in my previous pregnancies, the anxiety I felt with this one was magnified. Although my GP told me that the strength of the symptoms I was having was a good sign, she also couldn't reassure me that I wasn't going to lose this baby. I found this hard to bear. I know that medics can't guarantee anything, but someone like me who has massive anxiety levels needed that guarantee more than anything. Without it my anxiety increased. It was a vicious circle. I wasn't offered any early scans or extra reassurance at that time. I was told to just get on with my daily routine. Easier said than done when all you can think about is your current obsession and what may or may not be happening inside your body.

I think that if my worries had been taken more seriously, then maybe I would have been less anxious throughout this pregnancy. I should have requested an early scan – it would have been possible to carry one out at the EPU (as they had done to confirm the miscarriage). However, I didn't want to appear difficult. I was being compliant and not making a fuss. I took my empathic traits to a whole new level. The slightest feeling in my body that was new or different I attributed to my pregnancy. I didn't share these concerns with anyone; instead I internalised them and became quite withdrawn and distracted. I had awful nightmares and woke up shaking and sweating. I had bizarre dreams about faceless babies crying out to me, but I could never reach them. All in all, it was a difficult time... A stressful pregnancy that ended with a traumatic labour and birth.

Even though I had gone beyond the dreaded 13 week mark, I was overwhelmed by constant fear. I continued to become quite disconnected and introverted. My older daughter developed chickenpox during my pregnancy and this threw me into mass panic. I had never, to my knowledge, had chickenpox. I had heard of a distant acquaintance whose husband had caught it and died from complications. I had fixated on this, even though it is a rare occurrence, and developed a massive phobia about the disease. These extreme reactions are quite common in people with autism, but this was pre-diagnosis so I was just treated as an abnormally anxious person (in fact, the term 'hypochondriac' was used). I rang the hospital in a panic and they told me that they would perform a blood test to check my antibodies. The test came back showing that I already had the antibodies so I had either had a mild form of chickenpox in the past or I had come into contact with it at some point. This did placate me somewhat, although not entirely. I have since found out that there is a vaccine for chickenpox and I wonder why this isn't made routinely available in the UK. The reason I wonder about this is because I was to encounter the chickenpox problem again during my final pregnancy.

At my 20-week scan we were asked if we wanted to know the sex of the baby. This time round I was hoping for a boy as I couldn't shake off the feeling that I had lost a boy when I had the miscarriage. I was also worried that if we had a girl my older daughter would feel excluded. Her biological father, my ex-husband, only had contact with my sons and had not shown any interest in having contact with our daughter. My daughter looked on my second husband as her dad and he loved her as his own, but I was worried that if we had a daughter together then that would change his relationship with Charlotte. With this in mind, I decided that I did want to know the baby's sex. It was a girl. I was happy to have another daughter and felt blessed, but I was also a little worried. However, I needn't have been, because my daughters get on brilliantly and my husband treats them equally.

During the third trimester of this pregnancy I developed a painful throbbing sensation between my vagina and perineum. I had never experienced this before and made an appointment with the midwife. She told me that I had developed a varicose vein. I was slightly disbelieving because I thought you only got those in your legs! Apparently not. The main concern with a varicose vein between the vagina and perineum is that during the birth the vein can burst and cause heavy bleeding, which is difficult to stop. This was not the news that a highly anxious person needs to hear. The advice was to try and keep my legs elevated and keep pressure off that area. I embraced the excuse for lying down and watching television a lot. The problem was that the mere mention of the possibility of something happening translated in my mind as an absolute certainty. Black and white thinking. I spent a lot of time ruminating and worrying about the birth itself. Birth had not been easy for me with some of my children, but after the miscarriage I was truly terrified. As I approached the third trimester, I became more anxious than ever.

I was thankful at this stage in my pregnancy that I had decided to remain under the consultant's care. When I had first attended the antenatal clinic at my doctor's surgery the community midwife there had suggested that I have a home birth as my last labour had been so short. She did make quite a convincing case and I did seriously consider it. The thought of being in my own home and not having to endure the sensory overload of the hospital was very appealing. However, as I had given birth to all of my other children in hospital I was too scared to make a change, particularly after the miscarriage. I felt that I needed to be near medical equipment and obstetricians for the worst-case scenario. Since completing my doula training, though, I think that maybe if I had decided to stay at home with support then I may not have needed an emergency Caesarean section (C-section). But my mind was made up. Not going to hospital was change and I don't like change! I decided that I would go to hospital but this time I wanted my mother to be with me as well as my husband. My mother had been unable to attend my last birth and be my birth partner as planned because of her diagnosis of breast cancer and subsequent treatment. Now that she was in remission I knew that I wanted to share this experience with her.

At 38 weeks pregnant I attended an antenatal appointment. Throughout my previous appointments during this pregnancy I had usually had a problem with my observations: sugar in my urine; protein in my urine; slightly raised blood pressure one day but a little on the low side another day; I had a scan on my kidneys because of my erratic urine tests, which came back as normal. All in all, there was never a dull appointment… Until week 38. My urine was completely clear, my blood pressure was perfect and apparently my baby was in a good position. I left that appointment joking with my husband that the baby would probably be born that day. I didn't seriously believe that though because most of my other children except Matthew had been born later than my due date.

When I went to collect my other children from nursery and school, one of the other mums asked if she could feel my bump. I wasn't that comfortable with her doing it but I didn't feel able to say no. After a few awkward minutes she exclaimed that my tummy was tight and she felt sure that I would have the baby later that night. I told her that I didn't have time that day as I had to attend parents' evening.

At the parents' evening the head teacher was a little surprised to see me rocking on all fours outside a classroom while reading through my children's work. He did stop and ask if I was ok, and I replied that I was fine, nothing to worry about, baby not due for another couple of weeks. He rushed off, probably worrying that he would be called upon to deliver my baby if he stayed around any longer. I was sure it was just those pesky Braxton Hicks.

After the parents' evening I had a craving for something spicy so my husband and I stopped off at a local Indian restaurant. I was starving and ordered a large meal. I was extremely hypersensitive to the smells of the food and was near to drooling because I so wanted to satisfy that craving.

By the time the meal was served the smells had become revolting and I suddenly felt sick and couldn't eat anything. My back was aching and I was being bothered a lot by the Braxton Hicks pains I was experiencing. I couldn't stand to be in the restaurant any longer so I got up and waited for my poor husband to collect his food in a doggy bag so we could go home.

We arrived home, and my parents-in-law, who had been babysitting, looked at me and asked if I wanted them to stay just in case I needed to go to hospital. I reassured them that I was fine and sent them home. I went to bed confident that if I went to sleep the pains would stop because they weren't the real thing. I woke up in the early hours, relieved and a little disappointed to find I was no longer contracting. I got up to go to the toilet and for the first time ever I had a 'show' (plug of mucus from the opening of the cervix). I had only just managed to process that when I felt a pop in my tummy and a pool of water appeared at my feet. I shouted out to my husband that my waters had burst and then I went into panic mode. The last time my waters had broken naturally I had given birth within half an hour. I rang the labour ward at the hospital, who suggested I go immediately as my last labour had been so short. So my in-laws were called to return and stay with the children and my parents were called to meet us at the hospital.

As I waited for my in-laws to come and look after the children, my eldest son, James, came downstairs. Apparently, my shouting that my waters had broken had woken him up. He had turned ten years old the previous week and as I looked at him rubbing his eyes in his Aladdin pyjamas I was transported back to his birth and the first time I had looked into his eyes. I was overwhelmed with emotion and glad that I had been able to share that time with him before going to hospital.

Fortunately, the hospital was on the same road that we lived on so we didn't have far to go. All was going well. I was taken straight to the labour ward but I could feel my anxiety building again. White coat syndrome. The anxiety-provoking environment of the hospital was having a psychological effect on me. However, once my parents arrived, I began to feel much calmer.

The midwife looked through my notes and took my blood pressure, which was fine, but she didn't give me an internal exam. She told me that I should just push when I was ready and she was sure that we would have a baby by 9am. This was at 5.30am. As the labour progressed I mentioned that with my other children I had back labour and I was worried that this was why I had the urge to push. She reassured me and told me that I was doing well. A change of shift came and went and another midwife took over. Concerned about the lack of a baby this midwife examined me and told me to stop pushing immediately. I was only 3cm dilated and a lip had formed. I was crushed. This took me right back to my first labour and I began to panic.

I had gas and air for pain relief but refused an epidural as I had developed a phobia after I had one with my first baby. I had previously experienced an unpleasant reaction to pethidine so that was also ruled out. After some hours of this I began to shut down. I was in more pain than I had ever been in before and I just knew something wasn't right. Other women on the spectrum that I have spoken to since have also said how they are hypersensitive to their body and knew when things aren't right. I begged the doctor for a general anaesthetic and a C-section but my hysterical request was refused. I remember in the midst of what to me felt like torture looking towards my husband and he was eating a sandwich. It was in that moment I truly understood the urge to kill.

Eventually, after nearly a full day in labour the obstetrician decided to carry out a C-section as they had discovered at some point during my labour that my baby was transverse (lying sideways). They refused my request for a general anaesthetic. I would have much preferred this to an epidural, which was the usual procedure. I really did not want an epidural; I just wanted to be sent to sleep and to wake up when it was all over. I cried, begged and swore but I was told that there was no way they would give me a general anaesthetic so there was no point in me continuing to ask for one. I was eventually given an epidural and within minutes of it taking hold I was like a different person. Gone was the possessed, screaming wild woman and in her place was a pain-free, calm, coherent one.

At this point I was taken off to theatre. The sensory overload was unbelievable…the bright lights and loud noises but nobody talking to me. The one sound that I could hear constantly was my own heartbeat on the monitor in the operating theatre. Every now and then it slowed down and I was convinced that my heart was stopping; yet as I looked at the medical staff, none of them seemed to notice, which should probably have indicated to me that this was normal and I wasn't actually dying. It was a very traumatic experience. My daughter was eventually born safe and well at 6.13pm.

Hospital policy where I gave birth advised that if you had a C-section, you had your own room on the postnatal ward. This was a light at the end of the tunnel for me…until I was told that the wards were so busy there were no single rooms so I would have to stay in a six-bed ward. I was beyond upset.

I am fairly certain that whoever invented hospitals was not on the autism spectrum. When would it ever be a good idea to put people who are at their most vulnerable from the sheer nature of being in a hospital all in a big room together?

At first I couldn't move because I was still under the effects of the epidural, and when they wore off I still couldn't move because I was hooked up to a drip. The ward was extremely short-staffed and I had to wait long periods of time just for a bedpan or for someone to hand me my daughter when she cried. I had to sit with the curtains open because I couldn't get up to shut them, and I felt like a sideshow at the circus when everyone else's friends and relatives came to visit. I am sure they weren't really looking at me as though I was something out of the ordinary but this was my perception and that is what is important. I had been through the worst experience of my life to date and now I had to be in a room with lots of noise and lights, alongside people I didn't know plus their crying babies and visitors. It was horrendous. I began to experience the visual disturbances associated with migraine but instead of recognising what these were I panicked because I thought I was dying. The migraines were down to the stress of the experience I had been through and then not having my own room, a safe haven where I could retreat and calm down.

My daughter was born on a Thursday, and two days later – on the Saturday – I informed staff that I was going to discharge myself from hospital. I couldn't bear to stay there for another minute. The midwifery staff could see that I was having a bad time in hospital and they agreed to suggest to the doctors that they should let me go. In one way I was lucky because we lived so close to the hospital and I could be back there within minutes if necessary.

The children had made 'Welcome Home' banners, which they had strung to the door with daffodils from the garden. A lovely touch but I felt disconnected from everything. I think this was due to the transition from hospital to home as well as the experience I had been through. An emergency C-section is just that – an emergency operation whose main aim is to get the baby out quickly and safely. Having never been through this before I was unaware that it would have an effect on my emotions postnatally. I became extremely withdrawn after my daughter's birth and developed post-traumatic stress disorder. I sought help from a volunteer helpline and the lovely lady I spoke to suggested that I contact the maternity department and go back to the hospital to have a debrief of the birth experience. I did this and found it somewhat helpful, but I didn't have the energy in me to look at ways in which my care could have been different or articulate to the hospital where I thought things could have been improved in my care.

This time in my life became very dark. I had nightmares and panic attacks. Looking back now I think that I had held everything together for so long that my emotional reserves were now empty. I was heading towards a big meltdown. Finally, this birth experience had tipped me over the edge. It was this feeling again of not being listened to and not having any control over what was happening to me. With hindsight I think that the panic at losing control made the labour worse. I was trying to articulate my genuine fears and feelings and I felt that nobody was listening to me or taking my feelings seriously. I felt that I had failed by having a C-section, even though it was necessary and it became apparent during the debrief that the staff looking after me felt that my daughter was not going to be born naturally due to her position in the womb. I just became completely overwhelmed with life, and this started a downward spiral with my mental health. This is probably the reason why it took ten years for me to seriously contemplate having another child.

HELPFUL HINTS

If you are a highly anxious Aspie, try not to bottle up your feelings and anxieties. Offload them using whatever method is comfortable for you (for example, writing, drawing, recording or whatever it is you usually do to unburden yourself).

The physical recovery following my C-section was also hard. I had to remind myself that I had undergone major abdominal surgery and deal with the issues that came with that. The day after I returned home from hospital I got undressed to have a bath and was shocked at the sight of my body. I looked as though I had been involved in a car accident. I had large purple and yellow bruises around my stomach and I was shaken as I looked at myself. Due to the surgery I couldn't drive for six weeks because the wound needed to heal and my car insurance wouldn't cover me if I had an accident. This made me feel even more isolated and lonely. I became scared to go out for a walk with the baby as I found the traffic noises too much and I didn't like to be around people.

The community midwife came in regularly but due to her workload those visits were fleeting. My husband had returned to work. My mum came to see me as much as she could but since she had been diagnosed with cancer she had lost her confidence and stopped driving so she was reliant on public transport. Therefore, I spent a lot of time at home alone with my baby. I used to wait eagerly for the midwife to come but the visit was over quickly and I didn't feel as though I had the right to demand more time from her.

Meanwhile, I was having the same problems with breastfeeding as before and this time I switched fairly quickly to using formula. I had resigned myself to the fact that I was unable to breastfeed. I felt there was something in my body that was not working properly and despite everyone saying that all women could breastfeed I was certain that actually not all women could. I became quite irritated with the literature that suggested that breastfeeding was best and became quite anti-breastfeeding. I took the 'Breast is Best' slogan quite personally and felt that it was directed at me. It was only through completing the doula course that my feelings towards breastfeeding changed.

My new baby daughter was very much like my eldest son. She was calm and what would be considered a 'good' baby. I adored her but found it different being at home with just one child. I had been used to having at least two or three children running around and keeping me on my toes. I found my thoughts drifting towards studying or working. I loved reading to my daughter – well to all of my children – and I loved interacting with her, but I felt as though my brain was seizing up. I had a very short attention span when it came to playing with her – in fact, I found that aspect of mothering difficult and always had done.

I began to feel restless again, but I certainly wasn't contemplating another pregnancy. At that stage I felt that my special interest in having babies was well and truly over. I spent a lot of time on the Internet when my daughter was asleep. I had a new interest: I was searching for suitable academic courses or employment, but I kept hitting a brick wall. Studying was expensive and I still had some barriers to overcome with formal education as it hadn't worked too well for me in the past. However, I felt as though I hadn't fulfilled my academic potential and this was something that bothered me. I was torn because I didn't want to lose my connection with my children by working full time but I did feel as though I needed validation that I could achieve something in my own right.

I had been working evenings, weekends and some nights ad hoc for a funeral services company before and during my last pregnancy. This fitted in with the children and involved me taking phone calls from families, police and hospitals to arrange for funeral directors from across the UK to go and collect the deceased from where they had died and take them to the funeral home for preparation. I gained a great amount of satisfaction from this job. I enjoyed helping and supporting people in their time of need. I also enjoyed the interaction with police, hospitals and coroners. As I began to lean towards returning to work on a more regular basis, I found myself drawn towards the world of bereavement. Employment within that field was limited but eventually I telephoned a local undertaker who invited me for interview and offered me a job. I was ecstatic. I was successful at something that was outside my own home life. I was to remain within that industry until my mental health issues resurfaced with a vengeance.

As much as I loved my work, what I didn't realise at the time was that I was giving so much to the bereaved families that I worked with it was taking a toll on my mental health. Through my research and work within the field of autism I have discovered that this is very common for many women on the spectrum. We are like feelings sponges that soak up all the emotions we are exposed to. Interestingly, I found it much easier to work with the deceased than I did with my colleagues. With the former I didn't have to work out complicated social nuances and I could just go about my rewarding job in peace. Sadly, though, I also had to work with my colleagues in the land of the living. For reasons I didn't understand then, this began to cause me lot of stress. I was so anxious about how they perceived me that I was having regular panic attacks when I left work. My misunderstanding of social conventions meant that I also took everything my co-workers said to me very much to heart. I would wake up at night revisiting conversations and wondering what someone had meant by something they had said. Living like this was exhausting and I felt as though I was going insane.

My job was also very demanding. There was no second chance to get things right. A funeral was a one-day, make-or-break situation. I was constantly going over in my mind all the arrangements I had made at work. Had I covered everything and made sure that the funeral would go without a hitch? I often woke up in the middle of the night worrying about whether I had booked the organist for a funeral service or the gravedigger for a burial. I had nightmares that families would arrive at the cemetery only to find that the grave hadn't been dug because I had forgotten to arrange it. I'm happy to report that nothing like that ever went amiss – well, certainly not at any of the funerals I arranged.

The world of funeral directors at that time was very male-dominated – much more so than appears to be the case now – and I found this hard to cope with. I had always had difficulties in relationships with men and was now very wary of men in general. There were some men that I could relate to but they were usually the non-threatening type. I can't describe how I knew they were non-threatening; it was just intuition. Then there were the men that I found intimidating and with whom I struggled to interact without becoming anxious. All of this emotional turmoil was wearing me down and what with trying to be a perfect wife and mother as well it was only a matter of time before things would come to a head.

Eventually, following the arrangement of a baby's funeral and also that of an old school friend, I had a breakdown. I took some sick leave but it became apparent after a while that I would not be returning to work. I developed such a phobia about the building that I used to work in that I couldn't even work my notice. My husband had to return my office keys because I had an anxiety attack at the very thought of going into my old workplace. It wasn't far from where I lived and so I even had to take a longer, alternative route if I was going to the town centre – all because I couldn't bring myself to drive past the building. At the time I thought I was failing at life again. Other people could do these things without such adverse reactions. What was wrong with me?

The nightmares had returned and I was constantly worrying about my health. I would wake up in the night and be certain that I was dying. I would get out of bed, convinced that my heart had stopped beating. Sounds mad, I know (how would I have been able to get out of bed if my heart was no longer beating?!), but it felt so real to me. I was struggling to maintain a grip on reality and I felt like a disaster zone. I had given up a job, parts of which I had loved. I had been good at it, too (I had regular thank you cards and gifts from the families I had worked with). My children were now all in school so I was rattling around the house trying to do domestic chores and regularly visiting the doctor with minor ailments. Occasionally, I would have a fleeting thought that another baby would keep me safe at home and give me an excuse not to engage with society by finding employment. Fortunately, my husband could see that my mental health was deteriorating and that another pregnancy was not going to help.

One day I woke up from another nightmare and sat up in bed suddenly. The room was spinning. I had to grab the side of the bed because I felt as though I was going to fall off. I began to panic. I had never experienced anything like this and I was certain that it was something sinister. I shouted out for my husband, who came rushing to see what was wrong. I explained how I felt and he tried to calm me down, suggesting that it was probably a virus. I was sure it wasn't. I lay down and tried to stop the feeling of nausea as my head continued to spin. This spinning sensation continued throughout the day, but I refused to contact the doctor. I had spent so much time at the surgery over minor things but when something really did need medical attention I was terrified of going in case they told me I was dying. After a day or so the spinning lessened although it didn't disappear completely until a couple of weeks later when I woke up and it had gone. This was my first episode of vertigo but unfortunately not my last.

At this time I was a parent governor at my children's school. One day the head teacher asked me if I'd like to work a few hours a day as a classroom assistant and lunchtime supervisor. I thought long and hard about it as I was still feeling wobbly after my last job and my experience of vertigo. I discussed it with my family and we felt that getting me out of the house for a while was probably a positive thing. Finally, I decided that, yes, I would like to do that. I was very familiar with the school and the staff so it didn't feel too daunting. I ended up working within the speech and language class with a small group of children who were pre-verbal and had autism. I fell in love with this job and those children. I had a desire to make a connection with them and enter into their world. In a way I identified with them but at the time I didn't know why. I went from working ten hours a week to staying for longer periods and helping in class as a volunteer. I adored this work. I felt as though I had found my new vocation. I never thought I would be as passionate about a field of work as I was about bereavement, but it happened. It has to be said, though, that I miss working in funeral services to this very day.

As my passion grew I began to research further training within the field of autism and special needs. Then one day I saw a position for a teaching assistant to work with children with special educational needs (SEN) at my old primary school. I was intrigued and curious about returning to my old school so I applied for the position. I was given an interview and offered the job on the spot. I had come full circle. My parents lived a short distance from the school, which really hadn't changed an awful lot in 20 years. In fact, one of the teachers who had taught me was still there! (After taking the job it took me two terms to call him by his first name because I still viewed him as my teacher.) The school still smelled the same, and as I am hypersensitive to smell this gave me joyful sensory feedback and transported me to a familiar childhood place. The smell was a mixture of disinfectant, rubber plimsolls and its own unique school smell. This was such a happy time in my life. I loved the school I worked in and I felt as though I was actually making a difference to the children that I taught.

My children had settled well at their own school and I was looking into continuing my education at college. With the support of the school I applied for a place to become a qualified teaching assistant. I was successful in obtaining a place and was optimistic for the future.

I began college in the following September but as I left school to attend my first lecture I began to feel strange. I now call this feeling 'wrong in my skin'. I began to feel alone and disconnected and just 'wrong'. I hesitated about driving to college and desperately wanted to turn round and go home. Then I thought about work and how much trouble I would get into if I didn't go.

I managed to calm down enough to get into the city centre where the college building was located. I parked and walked across to the college. As I approached, a group of younger students came out of the door and I began to feel anxious. I entered the building and followed the group of people who were heading to the lift. I knew which room I was supposed to be in. Relying on my hypervigilance to get me there safely, I noted the floor I needed and went up in the lift. I arrived at the right floor and approached the classroom. As I entered I felt as though everyone was staring at me, and I was hot and shaking. I sat at the nearest table and kept my head down, refusing to make eye contact with anyone. The lecturer came in and we got started. By the end of the session I was feeling better and looking forward to returning the following week. I felt excited and enthusiastic about the modules of work we would be studying. Unfortunately, every week for the year of the course I experienced the same panicky feelings on my way to college. Some days I would feel so bad that I didn't attend at all. I was struggling with the assignments as they all seemed vague to me.

I now know that I am not unintelligent but at that time I felt very stupid. I knew the information that the assignments required; I just couldn't get it from my head onto paper. If it hadn't been for the support of my family and some of the other students attending the course I would never have got the qualification. But I did and it was one of the proudest moments in my life when I was awarded my certificate at the graduation ceremony, with my parents and husband in the audience. I had fallen in love with education again. I had always enjoyed learning, as long as I was interested in the subject; it was just everything else that came with it, such as social interaction and putting ideas to paper, that I found challenging. I wondered about completing a course through distance learning. Maybe that would be more suited to my learning style. It would certainly rule out the need to interact with other students.

At the school I worked in we began to have an increasing number of children in school who were diagnosed with autism, and so I started to work closely with the specialist autism team who were part of the local authority. The more I worked with them, the more passionate I became about autism. My interest had been sparked in my first job but now I became consumed with learning more. I enrolled on a distance learning course with a local university and found this extremely interesting. I became convinced that working for the outreach autism team was my ideal career. It was my dream job. Unfortunately, it was everyone else's as well because no vacancies came up for quite a while…until one day the autism practitioner from the local authority team came to visit and mentioned that someone was leaving the team. This was what I had been waiting for. I emailed the team manager and sent her my curriculum vitae. She emailed me back and this set off a chain of events that resulted in me joining the team that I had aspired to be part of. I did have to meet her a few times and exchange a few emails before I could actually make the leap of applying for the job. I was worried about the change, and I had reason to be. The effect of changing jobs and other changing circumstances in my life had a big effect on me.

I began my job with the Communication Autism Team (CAT) on 7 September 2008. In the summer I had been on holiday to Malta, where I had unfortunately fallen down a pot-hole and snapped a tendon in my ankle. So I started my dream job limping around on crutches. The team worked in different areas at that time and I was to be working in the east of the city. This was not the best news for me as I don't have a brilliant sense of direction and I only like to go to places that I am familiar with unless I have someone else with me. At the same time my eldest son was due to go off to university. This combination of situations caused me to have another breakdown in my mental health. I became more and more withdrawn and unhappy. I struggled to attend meetings at work or make visits to my schools. I felt out of my depth with my job and travelling across the city was stressful for me. I didn't want to disclose this to the managers at work as I thought they would think badly of me. I also missed my eldest son desperately – the house felt strange without him.

Within two months I was off sick and had been referred to the mental health team through my GP. I was told by them that I had depression again and was offered medication. By this time I felt that I had no alternative but to take it. I know now with the benefit of hindsight that I no longer wanted to be in my life and that there was a very thin line between me continuing or ending my own life. I had only seriously considered suicide before when my marriage broke down. Since that time, although I had struggled with periods of depression and anxiety, I had not been as low as I was at this time. It was only through a chance meeting with a locum psychiatric nurse who recognised that I had traits of Asperger syndrome that I received my diagnosis. I had experienced too much change and that on top of the difficulties I had faced throughout my life had pushed me into a breakdown.

My younger son, Daniel, had been going through the process of diagnosis for 18 months. He had suffered with some speech and language difficulties as a toddler but was eventually discharged by the speech and language therapy team. He didn't respond to his name and was diagnosed with glue ear and fitted with grommets when he was five. However, the grommets didn't seem to help with his response to verbal communication and he was discharged from the hearing clinic as his hearing tests were all fine.

He had always been different to my other boys: it was hard to connect with him, but I put that down to the fact that he had been so young when his father had left that maybe it had affected him more than his brothers. However, he was extremely bright and very verbal so he didn't attract too much attention at school, except for his behaviour. He would often answer back to the teachers and they would suggest that he was being rude. I felt instinctively that actually he wasn't being rude because that didn't fit in with how I saw him but then I worried that maybe I just didn't want to see it.

On one occasion a teacher complained to me about his attitude during a maths lesson. I knew that, unlike me, he was excellent at maths. When we got home I asked him what had happened. He told me that the teacher had been demonstrating a sum on the whiteboard and she had miscalculated so he told her it was wrong. She told him off for being rude but he was adamant that she had got it wrong and he was quite vocal about it. I discussed with him the fact that it was important to listen to the teacher, but he was equally unwavering in his belief that she had got the sum wrong and he had to point it out.

I decided to take my son to the GP, who referred him to a paediatrician. Eventually, after a full, multi-agency assessment he was diagnosed with Asperger syndrome.

I mentioned my son's diagnosis to the CPN who had spotted traits in me, and we discussed the possibility of an assessment for me. He himself was unable to carry it out as he wasn't qualified, but I was referred on to a private consultant psychiatrist who specialised in making adult diagnoses of autism. I also began a course of anti-anxiety medication. I am still on a maintenance dose of that today and I think it has saved my life. I no longer experience the physical symptoms of anxiety that I did before: the feeling of my nerve endings being exposed to the world, a jangling feeling as though my teeth were constantly on edge and the terrifying vertigo that debilitated me for periods of time. Following my own assessment and subsequent diagnosis I felt a massive sense of relief. I wasn't a failure. I was wired differently. I have heard other adults talk about their diagnosis and everyone has mixed feelings – some good and some not so good. For me it was a light bulb moment. I finally had an answer and it was one that I could accept. My diagnosis enhanced my work within the outreach team and I began to specialise in autism and girls. My manager and the whole team were extremely supportive around my diagnosis and one of my close colleagues sent me a 'congratulations on your diagnosis' card.

Chapter 8

HARRISON

So it was at this time in February 2010 that my husband and I began to discuss the possibility of having another baby. We discussed it in a light-hearted way initially. I was approaching 40 and it seemed to me that my family wasn't complete. I was happy in my work and I felt that my mental health was being managed. I guess the biological clock was also ticking away (although I still don't feel that I have completed my family even now). My husband and I decided that if I hadn't become pregnant within a year of trying, then it wasn't meant to be.

One month later, a few days before my period was due, I had a horrible metallic taste in my mouth that wouldn't go away. On the day my period was due I bought six home pregnancy tests that can give you a result from the first day of your missed period. The first one was positive. I wasn't sure that I had read the instructions properly because I can get confused when following instructions. It had also been a long time since I had done a pregnancy test. So just to be sure I did another one. It was positive again. I was pregnant, elated and scared at the same time.

The next day I made an appointment at the doctor's and told her that I thought I was pregnant and would she be able to do a test to confirm it? She asked me if I had done a home test and I said that I had. In fact I had done seven (I had been out to get one more – a different brand – just to be sure). I told her they were positive and she said she didn't actually need to carry out a urine test to confirm the pregnancy. The home tests were now so sophisticated that they were highly unlikely to be wrong – how times had changed! She told me to come back in a few weeks to fill in the paperwork for referral to the midwifery team. Everything seemed very laid-back, not what I had been used to previously. So I left feeling mildly deflated. I wanted to jump up and down and tell the world because at 40 I had thought that I would struggle to become pregnant. There was no doubt that I was pregnant though – my period start date had come and gone, I was exhausted, I felt sick and I was an emotional wreck.

I began to worry that something was wrong with the baby because I was classed as an older mother. The anxiety demon had returned. In fact, it had never really left – I think it had just been on a sabbatical. I became so fixated on the idea that there was a problem that I went for the first of two private scans. Like many people with autism, I see things as very black and white – good or bad with no in-between, no grey area. As I sat in the waiting room with my husband, I was nearly in tears, convinced that something had happened to the baby. If you haven't experienced this kind of anxiety, it can be hard to understand. So if you're reading this because you are supporting someone who is pregnant, you need to try to imagine how overpowering this feeling is. My husband kept telling me to 'stop worrying.' Not the best thing to say because if I could stop worrying that easily then I would have done so. Did he think I wanted to be worried?

When we went in for the scan I explained to the radiographer that I had an autistic spectrum condition and that I was highly anxious. She was excellent. She slowly explained every procedure and as soon as she found my baby's heartbeat she pointed it out to me and played it so that I could hear. It was an amazing moment and I felt elated that everything appeared to be ok. At only six weeks pregnant my baby had a strong and steady heartbeat. This was wonderful news. I was sent off with a CD of my scan and I left feeling happy and reassured that all was well. I played the CD to my children, to my parents and repeatedly to myself when I was home alone.

That feeling of contentment lasted for about three weeks. Then I became anxious again. I didn't have a window in my tummy so I couldn't check that my baby was still hanging in there. I began to ruminate about what might have gone wrong. I told myself that at the time I had the scan all was well, but what if something had gone wrong in between? I tried to reassure myself that my early stage symptoms were very strong and for me that was a good sign. I was eating crystallised ginger and wearing anti-sickness wrist bands to try to combat the nausea. I was dashing to the bathroom regularly and I was feeling highly emotional. All good signs, in a way. This didn't stop me from beginning to obsess about miscarriage and so I decided to make an appointment for another private scan. This time I went alone. I knew that my husband would think I was overreacting and that I should just relax, but I couldn't. He didn't understand my reactions and anxieties even though I had given him books to read on autism and Asperger syndrome. He just couldn't relate to those feelings. Again, this appointment was handled really well and after checking in on my baby again I was fine.

Unfortunately, like before, this feeling of relief didn't last long. In the back of my mind I kept remembering the miscarriage and reliving it in my head. I developed an obsession with needing to check on the baby but couldn't afford to keep paying for private scans so I hired a foetal Doppler. This meant that any time I felt particularly anxious, I could have a listen to my baby. I can't describe how much this eased my anxiety throughout my pregnancy. I think it also helped me to bond with my boy. I would lie on the bed and listen in to him and talk to him, telling him how much I loved him and couldn't wait to meet him.

HELPFUL HINTS

Consider hiring or purchasing a foetal Doppler. I hired mine for a small monthly fee and then just sent it back when I had given birth. I cannot recommend this highly enough as a way of calming your anxiety and also checking that baby is ok.

Eventually, I had my first appointment with a midwife and I attended the local birthing centre. She took my details and then told me that because I had an emergency C-section with my last baby I needed to be placed under consultant care. This meant that I would be having my baby in hospital, not in the midwife-led unit that was closer to home. I didn't mind because, having had such a difficult time with my last pregnancy, I had decided to have an elective Caesarean.

With my first four children I had so-called 'natural' births. However, through the reflective practice I carried out during my doula training I realised that they weren't really natural at all. There had been medical interventions in every one of my pregnancies except the second one. I had always assumed that this was the norm and had never stopped to think that actually there might be another way. The doula training opened my eyes to the fact that birth should involve choice. I'm not suggesting that a hospital birth is wrong but I am advocating that a woman should be aware that hospital birth and medical intervention are not the only options. One choice is no choice.

In spite of my previous pregnancies, I was like a first-time mother at this initial hospital appointment. I was highly anxious and the long wait didn't help. Twenty years ago with my eldest child I had felt like the youngest woman in the waiting room. This time I felt like the oldest! I felt 'wrong' being there and that I should be back at work. That was my life; that was who I was. I have always found it difficult to multi-task and focus on more than one thing at a time. I couldn't correlate the two personas in my mind. Career woman and mum-to-be – it just didn't marry up. After much agitation on my part, I was called in to see a midwife who took lots of details and a history of my previous pregnancies. My husband remained in the waiting room, probably much to his relief. The midwife said that I also needed to have some blood taken. Fine, I thought, I'm ok with having blood taken, not a problem. What I had forgotten was that I am fine having blood taken as long as I don't watch the procedure. However, it had been such a long time since I had been in the position of having a blood test that I forgot about that and looked.

I was sent out to wait to see the consultant, by which time I was on sensory overload and feeling very much as though I wanted to run away. Then after another long wait the midwife called me back into a side room and said she needed to discuss something with me. I was shaking like a leaf as I was sure that she was going to deliver some dreadful news. She didn't indicate that I could ask my husband to accompany me and I didn't ask if he could come as I was too anxious to speak. The room that we went into was very small. I could feel the walls closing in on me and I thought that at any minute I would probably start to cry. What she actually wanted to do was discuss the tests that I could have because I was an older mother-to-be. Just what I needed to hear. She gave me some printed information, which I didn't really want. I had already decided that I wasn't going to have any diagnostic tests. I had bonded with my baby and I would love him or her as they were. I couldn't agree to an invasive test to check if my baby was 'normal' when I had a disability myself. I returned to my husband for yet another long and anxious wait.

By the time I went in to see the consultant I was at meltdown level. We had been at the clinic for three hours and I was seriously done with it all. I went in and told the consultant, slightly hysterically, that I wasn't having this baby vaginally. I wanted an elective C-section or I wasn't giving birth at all. I explained about my diagnosis of Asperger syndrome, my anxiety and my last labour and she still tried to convince me that this time would be different and I should have a vaginal birth. However, I was adamant and got very agitated and upset. In the end she could see that I was deadly serious and agreed that I could have an elective Caesarean. My husband had mostly stayed silent throughout this exchange.

Mainly, I think because he was embarrassed. Even though he knows about autism, he struggles to deal with understanding me and my needs so he prefers to stay out of situations that may look to others as though I'm being non-compliant and making a fuss. I regret having nobody there to discuss my choices with rationally and who would advocate for me. That is not to say I would have decided on a vaginal birth after discussion, but if I had been able to discuss it with someone I trusted who was also informed and didn't have their own agenda, then maybe I would have reconsidered. Uninformed choice is no choice at all.

I really didn't enjoy my final pregnancy because I was just so worried that something would go wrong. Whilst writing this book and reflecting on that time again, I was drawn to the idea that having a doula would have helped me. Having met some wonderful women who are doulas or who are training to become doulas, I know that although having had one wouldn't necessarily have changed any of my personal outcomes it would certainly have decreased my anxiety levels.

The second trimester in this pregnancy presented a challenge that I hadn't experienced before. Between weeks 24 and 28 mums-to-be may be offered a test for gestational diabetes (GD). Depending on where you are geographically this can be routine or it may be offered if you are at higher risk of developing the disorder by having a family history of diabetes. I had no family history and had never been diagnosed with GD in my other pregnancies. So off I went, for the first time ever not assuming the worst as I was certain my test would be fine. What I hadn't realised was that my inability to get round the supermarket without stopping to pick up a bottle of glucose drink and then finish it before I got to the checkout could possibly be a symptom of GD. I hadn't realised that my intense agitation and irritation with absolutely everything could be a symptom of GD. I also hadn't worked out that feeling constantly exhausted and falling asleep, then jerking awake with dribble running down my cheek, could also be a symptom of GD. I was oblivious.

The best part of attending hospital for the GD test was when I saw the boxes of glucose drinks stacked up. As soon as I saw them I was desperate for a bottle or six. I managed to get through the test and was told to telephone for my results later that day, which I did. I wasn't actually paying that much attention when I telephoned for the results. I was trying to pull myself together from another impromptu nap before collecting my daughter from school. I had to ask the midwife to repeat herself because I couldn't quite believe that the results were positive. The midwife repeated that, yes, my results showed I had GD and that my pregnancy had just become 'high risk' (not the best thing to say to an older mum-to-be with a diagnosis of an autism spectrum condition and anxiety disorder). I went to collect my daughter and sat in the car with tears running down my face. This was just another problem and worry to add to my already bulging sack of them.

I had been given a date to attend the diabetes clinic at the hospital the following week. My consultant would also change to one who specialised in the care of mothers with diabetes. I looked at everything I could find on the Internet about GD before I went to the clinic. The appointment came and I was told a little bit about diabetes and the implications it had for my pregnancy and birth. I was instructed on how to test my blood sugars and record them in a book. Fortunately, my husband was with me because I couldn't remember how to use the glucose meter and what my blood sugar levels were meant to be. The thought of pricking my fingers ten times a day terrified me because of my hypersensitivity to touch, but there was no other alternative. I was told that I would probably just need to make alterations to my diet throughout my pregnancy to manage the diabetes. I felt slightly happier about that because I didn't really relish the thought of injecting insulin.

I went home and spent the next week trying to wean myself off my glucose drink of choice. This was not easy. I attended my next appointment with my diary of glucose readings only to be told that the diet wasn't working so I would need to take insulin. I became agitated and upset. I explained to the diabetes nurse that I had an autism spectrum condition and was highly anxious and that I couldn't possibly inject myself. The alternative was to take medication in tablet form. I didn't really like the sound of that either as there were some side-effects to consider.

Following a discussion about the pros and cons of both forms of medication, I decided that the insulin injection would be the better option. The nurse was helpful and reassuring and went through the procedure with me a few times, taking time to explain and answer questions. She also gave me a number to telephone and said I could call whenever and as often as I needed to. I was also to contact her by telephone on a weekly basis to give her my blood sugar readings so she could see if the amount of insulin I was using was correct.

This was hugely helpful and I think being able to say that I was on the autism spectrum helped her to understand just how anxious I was. The irony of this is that for the rest of my pregnancy I found the routine of testing my blood sugar levels and taking insulin quite calming. It was rigid, time-measured and routine-based. In fact, after my son's birth I no longer had to test my blood or take insulin and I missed that routine.

My baby's due date was (according to my dates) 31 December 2010. The date was then changed by the hospital to 9 January 2011. This caused me a problem. I had given birth to all of my children in even years: 1990, 1992 and so on. This was extremely important to me. As rigidity and repetitive behaviours are a part of autism I couldn't contemplate having a baby in an odd year. In my mind I felt that to do so would be wrong and unlucky. Many people with autism have similar fixations on even, odd or prime numbers. Routine and repetition are very important to us and make us feel safe. Because of this I felt strongly that I could not have a baby in an odd year. It is important for people to understand this about autism. It is a compulsive feeling, not a bizarre or wacky idea. Nonetheless, my protestations fell on deaf ears. The hospital scan machine, which had not been present at the conception of my son, was right and I was wrong. No one could understand my rigid thinking around this, the fact that I needed my son to be born in an even year. It wasn't a whim, it was a genuine *need.*

Despite all of this, I had decided to work up until the Christmas break, which was 21 December, and start my maternity leave then. This would hopefully distract me from my due date, maybe encourage my baby to be born in the right year and also give me more time with him during my maternity leave. Unfortunately, the GD had other ideas. I was regularly attending the diabetes clinic but it was difficult to get the insulin levels right. I kept experiencing a huge drop in my sugar levels, which in turn made me feel extremely ill and I was advised not to drive.

I eventually decided to begin my maternity leave in October. I was upset at the thought of having less time with my baby after he was born but I was also relieved as I felt so ill. To compound the situation, towards the end of the second trimester I developed symphysis pubis dysfunction (SPD). This is pain in the pelvic region that is caused by stiffness or misalignment of the pelvic joints. I guess this was not surprising as I had carried five good-sized babies before, but the pain was awful. I couldn't turn over in bed properly and I eventually had to use crutches – not the best thing for someone as uncoordinated as me. I had to attend physiotherapy and was shown exercises to do. In addition, I was given a belt to support my bump. With my heightened sensory needs I found that the support belt irritated my hypersensitive skin. So I spent a lot of time researching alternative belts and eventually ordered one off the Internet. That turned out to be a waste of money because it also irritated me. In the end I resorted to using one crutch and holding my bump when I walked. I did think at the time that I would never walk properly again, but I am happy to report that three years on I am fine.

I was unable to attend any kind of antenatal class due to my anxiety in social situations. Over the years I had wasted so much money on gym memberships, it was ridiculous. I would join the gym with every intention of going but then I just couldn't face it. I became anxious at the thought of being around people I didn't know and I would get worried about where to go and what to do. What I really needed was to go there alone initially to orientate myself or have a buddy come and support me. A very good friend and colleague offered to accompany me to antenatal classes but unfortunately they were all in the day when she was working, so I didn't go. I liked the sound of yoga and swimming but aside from my concerns about social situations I didn't have the energy or the inclination to carry out these activities. The GD was taking its toll and I was just incredibly tired.

In my previous pregnancies as well I had been too anxious to consider going to any of these classes. Therefore, during most of my last trimesters I became very introverted and spent a lot of time ruminating about the worst-case birth scenario. This was a particular theme in my first and last pregnancies. I had no other children at home to concentrate on and no job to think about. I would mentally psych myself up to attend an antenatal class, get ready in time and have the intention of going, but as soon as it came to leaving the house I couldn't do it. The thought of walking alone into a room full of people was too overwhelming so I missed out on many things. I tried telling myself that in this latest pregnancy it wasn't my fault as the diabetes was having an adverse effect, but I think that even if I hadn't had this condition I would have found another reason not to go. Unless you experience those feelings yourself, it is extremely hard to understand them. As an antenatal doula I would offer to attend these classes with my client as a support person because I understand the trauma of attending them alone.

During this time spent at home in my final pregnancy I thought a lot about my birth options. I had been adamant that a C-section was the only way to go, but because I had so much time on my hands I now began to read about the risk factors, the for and against for vaginal birth after a Caesarean (VBAC), and the same for a second Caesarean. Having had an emergency C-section with Olivia, I was determined not to go through a long labour only to experience the end result of an emergency Caesarean again. In my heart of hearts I felt sure that this would happen.

My problem was my new consultant (not the one whom I had hysterically persuaded to agree to a Caesarean, but the one who specialised in the care of diabetic women). She was set on the idea of inducing my labour and giving me the chance to deliver vaginally. In the final trimester I had heated debates with her about what would happen. I was furious that I was being told what I was allowed to do and that I was putting my baby and myself at risk by wanting a C-section. On the other hand I was terrified that she was right and I was going to regret having the operation. It was a hugely difficult and confusing time and I had no independent support from anyone. My husband was siding with the consultant because he was worried about the effect a C-section would have on me and also he thought that there was no harm in trying to give birth vaginally and having a Caesarean as a last resort. He would think that – he had no idea of labour or of how anxious the whole thought of going through labour made me.

My mind drifted again to the possibility of hiring a doula. Although, the doula has been a theme throughout this book I had never heard of them until 2010 when I researched the role of a birth supporter and came across the description of a doula. I read this description with interest and thought about how one might help me. I also thought about what a wonderful job that would be. At this time I was still being told by the hospital that I would be having a vaginal delivery, so I felt that if that was the case I wanted someone with me as an advocate because I knew my husband wouldn't be able to act for me during the stressful and emotional time that is labour.

I do feel that women empower women and you only truly understand something if you have experienced it yourself. This doesn't mean that I don't think dads should be at the birth, but in my experience it's important to have another woman there who doesn't have an agenda. (My first husband wasn't at all empathetic during any of my pregnancies and labours; my second husband just felt helpless.) In fact, I had a visit from a lovely lady whom I would have employed as my doula had things worked out that way. I met with her and discussed my options. She had experienced a VBAC and we discussed that. She spoke to me about active labour and I went straight out and purchased a birthing ball, which I sat on daily.

As the weeks of my pregnancy passed, the GD was becoming more difficult to manage. I began to experience more dips in my blood sugar levels and I began to feel worse. I was still having regular appointments with the consultant and the diabetes nurse, and I was beginning to lose the will to fight with them anymore. I was on my way to handing my birth over to the medics again.

By 34 weeks I was still battling with the diabetes. I was still trying to fight my case for a Caesarean but my heart was no longer in it. I was attending weekly appointments and at week 37 the consultant gave me an internal examination to see if my cervix was favourable. She informed me that if it was, she was going to induce me the following week as the diabetes was becoming too hard to control. True to its rebellious nature my cervix was most definitely not favourable, so she sent me off with instructions to return the following week. This I did and we went through the same process with my cervix no doubt laughing to itself as it remained defiantly unfavourable. At this point we were on 21 December, the last week before the Christmas period. As the holidays were nearly upon us, the consultant told me that I had got my own way and grudgingly said that she would book me in for an elective C-section.

I was so relieved… No uncertainty about when I would have my baby, no looking for 'signs of labour'. I knew the exact date of delivery (and it was in an even year!), so I could set about planning for that. Of course, I'm not suggesting that all women on the autism spectrum should be given an elective C-section, but knowing the date my baby was going to be born certainly helped *me* to avoid the anxiety levels I had struggled with in my previous pregnancies. I found it very hard to understand the concept of a due date anyway. Having investigated further, I discovered that all of the literature states that only 4–5 per cent of babies are actually born on their due date. So how helpful is that? It seems obvious to me that a due date is more of a 'guestimate'. This is important to know if you are on the autism spectrum. I quite like the idea of having a 'due month' or 'due weeks'. That may not work for some people on the spectrum but having experienced issues surrounding a specific due date I think it would work better for me.

During the final trimester there is a lot happening both emotionally and physically as your body prepares for labour and birth. It is during the final trimester – especially the last few weeks – that the baby begins to gain more weight in readiness for existing outside the womb. I had become accustomed to all of my babies' movements throughout my pregnancies, noticing when they were active and when they were sleeping. My last baby's movements seemed very strong and there were a few times when they were actually quite painful. In fact, on one occasion I told the midwife that I was sure he had pinched me! This is because of the tactile hypersensitivity I experience. Even though I was aware that I was hypersensitive when the baby was moving, it wasn't the first thing I thought of. I imagined that there was something wrong when I found his movements unpleasant. Sometimes I felt quite panicky and sick… Those visions of aliens exploding felt a little more real.

With my latest pregnancy I had the diagnosis of Asperger syndrome and I assumed that this would empower me to make myself heard. I also thought that the medical staff that I would come into contact with would understand my needs. I have already described how in the third trimester the differences of opinion between my consultant and myself, and the uncertainty each week of not knowing if I would be induced or sent home, were difficult to deal with. I had embarked on this pregnancy with the hope that having a diagnosis would change my experience of pregnancy, labour and birth. In some ways it did. Certainly, it made me kinder to myself. I accepted the things I found difficult as part of my condition and didn't mentally beat myself up over things I found hard. However, I think the only difference it really made was to me. The reason it didn't make a difference to the care I received or the people I came into contact with is because of their lack of awareness. So, yes, I was kinder to myself but there was still that stigma of a hidden disability.

When the decision was finally made that the diabetes was no longer responding as well to the insulin as it had been and so I needed to deliver sooner rather than later, I was hugely relieved. I chose 23 December for my C-section and was told to arrive at the hospital the night before so that my blood sugars could be monitored overnight. On the day of the 22nd I tried to do some last-minute Christmas shopping, but couldn't make it round the supermarket due to the cramps I was having in my stomach. 'Aha,' I thought to myself, 'it's those Braxton Hicks again.' I was certain that they were more painful because I had been pregnant so many times. In the end I gave up trying to shop any more. I figured that the children would have a new brother for Christmas so what more could they possibly want! We went out for a lovely family meal (which in my negative state of mind I thought of as the last supper!).

Even though I had chosen my method of birth, I was still highly anxious. As I said goodbye to my older children I was convinced that I would never see them again as I was going to die during delivery. I cried all the way to the hospital and by the time I got there I was a nervous wreck. The midwives on the ward were lovely but, again, they were new to me. I had made almost weekly trips to the hospital for most of the third trimester but I still didn't recognise any of the staff on the ward. My husband finally left me there with my thoughts – bad news – and promised to return early the next morning. I tried to watch television but I couldn't concentrate. I could hear the noises of other women in labour and I became more anxious even though I knew that I wouldn't be labouring naturally. I had been told that I would go down to the delivery theatre first thing in the morning, so I tried to think positive thoughts. I also spoke to my unborn baby a lot. I told him that I couldn't wait to meet him and that he would have a calm entry into the world. The positive element to being in hospital overnight was that I had my own room. This contributed to lessening my anxiety.

First thing in the morning, a midwife came and introduced herself (another new face), and said that she would accompany me to theatre. Then the anaesthetist arrived brandishing a consent form and I felt my new-found bravery starting to crumble. He asked me if I had any worries to which I replied that, yes, I did have one particular worry. He asked me what it was and I said, 'I think I'm going to die.' There was a silence and I'm not sure whether he thought I was joking, but then he saw how upset I was and he asked me how long I had felt like that. I told him that I had felt like it all through the pregnancy (as well as through most of my life!). I explained about my Asperger's and he took the time to discuss the spinal block procedure and to try to reassure me. He also offered me the option of having a general anaesthetic if I was that scared of the spinal block. He told me that I could opt for that if I wanted, but obviously it would mean I would miss my baby's entrance into the world. I thought about it and decided that I did want to be awake when my son was born, so I opted for the spinal block. I am hugely grateful to that anaesthetist for taking the time to discuss the options with me and build a relationship. By doing so I had faith in him as he had gained my trust. He told me that he would see me in theatre and I would be well looked after. He was absolutely right.

I was able to walk down to theatre, albeit on legs that kept trying to walk the other way, and when I went through the door the radio was playing Christmas songs. I have to confess to sidling along the operating theatre walls – probably looking like a madwoman with my hospital gown and ghostly white face. The staff were friendly and said that they had heard I was a 'little nervous' (medic speak for 'terrified'), but they were going to look after me.

My first challenge was still the spinal block as I get so scared of anything going into my back. Despite the anaesthetist's earlier reassurances I was still frightened now that the reality of it all had hit me. I was told to lean forward and keep still (not an easy task when you've got a baby doing aerobics in your womb). I did it though and was helped to lie down as the anaesthetic took hold. Unfortunately, my anxiety took hold at the same time and I was convinced that the numbness was travelling up to my chest not down to my belly. I had visions of the anaesthetic numbing my heart (I'm not sure that's biologically possible but at that moment anything was possible as far as I was concerned). I started to cry and panic as they lay me down, so they sat me up again. The anaesthetist talked me through what was happening and calmed me down by getting me to focus on my breathing. My chest tightness began to disappear. I was slowly laid back down and the serious work began. The Christmas tunes were still playing and although I had bought my iPod and favourite music with me, I found myself focusing on the festive songs.

The medical team was amazing. They talked me through the whole procedure and even told me that had I not come in for the C-section, my baby would probably have been born that day or the next as his head was already engaged. That explained the contractions I had experienced in the supermarket. They had to use forceps to get his head out and after a short period of feeling as though someone was pulling me around the bed I heard a baby cry...my baby. The midwife brought him up to my chest and he was perfect. Despite the concerns about him being a big baby due to the diabetes, he was actually my smallest baby, weighing in at 7lb 2oz. I wasn't even aware that I was being stitched back together as I gazed at my gorgeous boy who looked a little disgruntled at having been woken up and removed from his warm cocoon. It was over and I was still alive.

As I was wheeled to recovery with my precious baby the staff jokingly said that as I had found it such a positive experience they would see me again in a year or so! I knew at that point I wouldn't be tempting fate again. This, my final birth, had been wonderful, positive and calm and that's what I wanted to remember. I was relieved that I felt that this was a good birth; and it had brought closure to my fifth birth, which had been so traumatic. I went into the recovery room feeling very blessed.

My son was placed skin-to-skin on me, which I found a wonderful experience. He snuffled around and found my breast and began to feed. I was so determined to breastfeed him. I felt sure that nothing could go wrong this time. I didn't have other toddlers to run around after, and I was older and more experienced, so this time breastfeeding would work. Holding my son skin-to-skin immediately after the birth was a totally new experience for me. It is recommended for babies to be close to their mums so they can continue to hear her heartbeat, and I found this to be a really positive experience.

Obviously, when a baby is born, it's all a bit messy. There's some blood and amniotic fluid and other secretions. For those mums with sensory challenges this can be a concern. It's important to consider how you want your baby to be handed to you. Some women want to hold their baby immediately, birth secretions and all. Others want their baby cleaned up a little first. There's no wrong or right way, it's down to personal choice. People who don't comprehend strong sensory sensitivities may not understand your decision. Therefore, it's important to be aware of this and discuss your feelings with whoever is going to be present at the birth, and also make a note of it in your birth wishes (birth plan). Personally, I wanted my babies cleaned up a little before they were given to me. This happened, but it was only with my last baby that I was offered the choice of holding him skin-to-skin.

We spent some time in recovery and then we were wheeled up to the ward and back to my own room. What a relief! No other people to interact with, no sensory overload. I was on a massive high. About 20 minutes later, the door opened and my other children came in. I will hold that memory with me for the rest of my life. They were thrilled with their new brother and we spent a lovely day in the hospital. My parents came later the same day and we had our very own birth party in my room. That night, after everyone had left, I looked down at my little miracle and thought that I couldn't be any happier.

My son had slept most of the day while he was being greeted by his family. I was told that this was probably due to the effect of the medications I had received during the Caesarean and also because he hadn't had to do any work himself to be born. However, this all changed later that evening. My little man seemed to spend a lot of time crying – well, screaming – unless he was in my arms. This was a difficult manoeuvre because the hospital rules stated that for safety reasons babies were not meant to be kept in their mother's bed while she slept. Because of my immobility from the spinal block and the abdominal wound, I had to request assistance every time I needed to get my son out of his bassinet. This meant that I was constantly pressing the nurse call button.

In the early hours of the morning one of the midwives suggested that she take him with her so that I could rest. I gratefully accepted her offer. Unfortunately, after she had taken him I still didn't get any sleep because I was worried that something would happen to him. I had images of him being abducted as he slept somewhere on the ward. I needn't have worried, though, because after less than an hour the midwife was back with a still crying baby, explaining that she couldn't placate him. She placed him in my arms and he nestled down and stopped crying. I breastfed him on and off but didn't call the staff back to put him in his cot. In fact, I was reprimanded in the morning because I had fallen asleep with my baby in my arms. I didn't care, I knew that I had not been in a deep sleep and I was consciously and acutely aware of my baby's movements.

It was Christmas Eve and I had the best gift ever. My family all visited again that day and after my older children had left and my parents were preparing to leave, a midwife marched business-like into my room. 'We are moving you to a ward now,' she said. I looked at her in disbelief. I really did not want to be moved. My contentment evaporated. She told me that she would be back soon, so could my family gather my belongings together. No one said anything. I could feel myself getting upset and, sure enough, I burst into tears. I was not moving. If I had to move, then I was discharging myself. I repeated this to my husband and my parents, who weren't quite sure how to deal with my increasing agitation. I started to pull at the cannula in my hand and demanded that my husband go and tell them that I wasn't moving. He stood in the room uncertain of what to do in the face of my sudden outburst. The midwife came back in and surveyed the scene around her. She wanted to know what the problem was. My husband explained that I didn't want to move to a ward. He didn't mention that I had Asperger's and I was unable to speak at that moment. She told us that they had a patient who was very poorly and needed a side room. My husband caved in and didn't argue. The midwife pushed my baby out of the room and told us to follow her, which we did. I was still silently crying at this point, but I followed behind reluctantly. She had my baby, what else could I do?

As we entered the ward, the first thing I saw was the other mothers and their families. They all stared as we entered the ward. For me that was the final straw. I went from crying and feeling submissive to aggressively pulling the tape holding my cannula in place and informing my family in a rather loud voice that I was going home. My husband tried to tell me that it was only for one night as hopefully I would be discharged on Christmas Day, but I was in no mood to listen to him. Even one night was too much in my opinion. The cannula was still in place and showing no signs of coming out so I started to fling my clothes into a bag. As I did this I was becoming more upset and angry.

Eventually, my lovely mum marched off in search of a midwife. Shortly afterwards she returned with one, who proceeded to patronise me by saying they couldn't put me back in the room I had just vacated as they had someone in there who was ill. I said in no uncertain terms that if that were the case, then fine, but I was discharging myself and my baby. She tried to tell me that to do that was inadvisable and if I suffered any problems then I had to accept responsibility. Fine, I was going home. She had obviously thought that I was bluffing and that she could talk me out of this nonsense of leaving. I think it was at this point that she realised maybe she couldn't and I was deadly serious. She left the ward as I continued to throw my belongings into my bags. She returned rather swiftly with another midwife and they said that they had found a room for me but it didn't have its own bathroom. That was ok. I could handle that. As they walked me back up the ward I had the distinct impression that they thought I was being ridiculous.

When we got into the single room I explained to the staff that I had Asperger syndrome, to which they replied, 'Oh yes, we saw that in your notes.' I didn't have the energy to pursue this comment at that moment but I made a mental note to educate medical staff in some way at some point in the future so that no other woman would have to go through the experiences I had. Hopefully, this is where this book can play a part. I am sure that the midwife wasn't deliberately being dismissive. I honestly think that there is still this idea that if you don't look like you have a disability then you don't have one. Many people still believe that autism doesn't exist or that to be autistic you have to be like the one person they have ever encountered or seen on the television who has autism. In my more belligerent moments I often think that those of us on the autism spectrum have got it right: we don't judge or try to label people. Maybe in years to come people will be diagnosed with neurotypical disorder…

So there I was, back in my room – with no toilet – and I still had the problem of dealing with a baby who would only stop crying if I held him in my arms. I was exhausted but I had no inclination to call the midwives back, because I didn't want them to think I was a complete incompetent. My husband and parents had left as soon as they were certain I was comfortable. They no doubt went for a well-earned drink somewhere. The pattern of constant crying continued. If I was holding my son, he was either feeding or asleep; but as soon as he was put into his cot, he would wake up screaming indignantly. I didn't mind initially – I was so euphoric at having him, I could have sat up with him forever. However, I was apprehensive about spending another night awake on account of not being allowed to fall asleep with him in my bed.

As midnight approached on Christmas Eve and I sat nursing my little angel, a different midwife came in with two Christmas presents. 'Santa has been,' she whispered. She handed me the gifts: 'One for you, one for baby, merry Christmas.' This was apparently a hospital tradition – everyone on the ward that night got a present. It was such a thoughtful touch. Unfortunately, it was slightly marred by my earlier experience, which had left me with a bittersweet feeling about the whole hospital situation. However, the night shift meant that new staff were on hand and I put the unpleasantness of earlier to one side while I concentrated on savouring the moment. I have always loved Christmas and this year I had received the best Christmas gift ever. As I unwrapped my son's first-ever Christmas present, I was certain that I could hear the faint sound of jingle bells outside.

Following another night with little sleep, where I had desperately tried to stay awake but had again fallen asleep with my son in my bed, I hoped that today I could go home. It was Christmas Day and I missed my other children and the rest of my family. I was also panicking in case the staff tried to move me onto a ward again. However, there was something to be said for a Christmas morning where I was brought breakfast in bed and wasn't supervising a mass gift-opening session. The paediatrician had checked my son the day before and he was fine; I was the one who needed to be checked over before discharge. There was certainly a much lighter air on the ward that day. I was told that there was a very high possibility that I would be discharged that day, which was excellent news. All of my observations were fine. I hadn't needed to check my blood sugars after giving birth and I was finding this transition a little bit difficult to cope with. I kept panicking because I hadn't checked my glucose levels, then realising that actually I didn't need to.

My husband and children came to visit a little later that morning and they brought most of our presents so we had a lovely morning opening our gifts together. While we were doing this, the midwife in charge asked us if we wanted to have Christmas lunch there as they had got some spare ones. We didn't hesitate in saying yes and so our Christmas Day in 2010 was spent on the maternity wing opening presents and eating turkey. It was surreal but actually wonderful.

I was eventually discharged at teatime. I returned home to a wonderful meal prepared by my husband and children, but not long after I got back I began to feel a little spaced out. I hadn't really felt like this in hospital this time. Yes, I had gone into meltdown over the move to a ward but this feeling was different. I didn't feel emotional, I felt disconnected. I initially put it down to the pain relief I was taking, but having examined the situation in retrospect I think it was more to do with transition from hospital to home. I often have problems when I get home from work, or after staying away at a conference, or returning from holiday. It also works vice versa. I have transitional issues when I go to hotels and when I return to work after the school holidays. But when I got home after giving birth, the feelings hit me like a tidal wave and I must have seemed very quiet to everyone. I was also in a lot of pain with my abdominal wound and I was beginning to feel the effects of lack of sleep. Over the holiday period I spent most of my time having what I can now call a 'babymoon'. The term 'babymoon' was something that I heard when I was completing my doula training. It is just like a honeymoon but it's time for you and your baby to spend getting to know each other and bond with each other.

I was determined to breastfeed completely and on demand. I co-slept with my baby and he fed whenever he wanted, day and night. However, when the midwife came to weigh him he wasn't gaining weight. I was horrified. How could this happen when I had done everything so differently this time? The advice was the same: top up with formula or express my own milk. I had a breast pump but, again, I was getting nothing out. It was with a very heavy heart that I began to top up with formula. My son didn't really appear to enjoy it, so I began to think that maybe he wanted to breastfeed but the problem was within me. I phoned helplines and read everything I could about breastfeeding. I was still breastfeeding on demand and co-sleeping with my son, but I couldn't continue solely with breastfeeding if he wasn't gaining weight. I eventually stopped offering him the breast at four months. I had been relying more on formula for those months but I continued to offer the breast because he seemed to enjoy it and so did I. (It was only through my doula training three years later that I finally found out the possible reason why I was unsuccessful at breastfeeding.)

Prior to my last pregnancy I had been taking anti-anxiety medication. I had started initially on 60mg daily but before I got pregnant I was only taking 5mg per day. I was desperately trying to come off medication as I thought it was the one thing that proved I couldn't cope with life. I went through my final pregnancy without taking anything for my anxiety, and following Harrison's birth I was adamant that I would not be going back onto medication. I was certain that I could cope, especially now that I had my Asperger's diagnosis.

I was very interested in attachment parenting and this fitted in with having a baby who appeared to be tactile seeking and hypersensitive to sound. Although my breastfeeding was not as successful as I had envisaged, I was still offering Harrison the breast for a comfort feed during the night. He slept in my bed, while my husband slept in another room. This was beneficial as it meant that my husband didn't get disturbed during the night when he had to get up for work early in the morning. As Harrison got bigger, I began to notice that he enjoyed being held and rocked and that he also loved the white noise app I had on my smartphone, or the sound of the hairdryer. All of those things would send him off to sleep. I was besotted with him.

I was due to go back to work when Harry was nine months old and I was dreading it. I had looked at some nurseries locally but I couldn't bear the thought of sending him. I was completely miserable. I had to go back to work for financial reasons, and I did love my job, but I didn't think I could stand the physical pain of separation from my boy. I initially went back to work for four days a week and my mother looked after him. I hated it. I was no longer working in the east of the city because my manager had been very accommodating and had changed my work area to be slightly nearer to home. This was helpful as it was close to where my parents lived and I could drop Harry off, go to work and then pop back at lunchtime. This became a good routine but I still missed him and craved being at home with him.

In the October before Harry turned two years old I woke up one day with vertigo. Instead of thinking rationally that I had experienced this before and it had gone, so this too would pass, I didn't. I went into full panic mode again. I became upset and anxious, and the more anxious I became, the more I think this fuelled the dizziness I was experiencing. I refused to go to the doctor's, thinking that they would tell me that I was seriously ill and I wouldn't live to see my baby grow up.

I was off work because I was so dizzy, but I just kept hoping that like before I would wake up and it would be gone. This time, however, it appeared to be hanging around.

In the end I did make an appointment at the doctor's. I sat in the waiting room and felt as though I had been given a death sentence, even though I hadn't even been in to see a doctor at that point. I was called in for my appointment, and when the doctor asked me what she could do for me, I burst into tears. I explained the vertigo and the thoughts and fears that accompanied it. She checked my eyes, ears, reflexes and motor responses and eventually said that my ears were full of fluid and this was affecting my balance and causing vertigo. I began to cry again, this time with relief. So I wasn't dying? 'Not today,' she replied kindly. I was given a nasal spray and sent home. Within a few days the vertigo had gone and it was like the whole scenario had been a bad dream.

I carried on juggling work with being a mum, but even though I thought I was fine, my husband and parents had noticed a difference in me. I didn't appear to be as calm as I had been immediately after Harry's birth. I was more irritable, angry and confrontational. I would often burst into tears for no reason and I had begun to spend more time lying in bed at weekends. My health was suffering and I was taking sick days off work more regularly due to minor ailments. I wasn't as engaged in my work as I had been and I had become lethargic. Although a few years earlier I had stopped attending social events unless I really wanted to go to them, now I was refusing to leave the house to go *anywhere*.

I wouldn't go to restaurants that we occasionally went to as a family and I became obsessed with what I was eating. As had been the case 20 years previously, this was nothing to do with weight loss; it was to do with paranoia about getting food poisoning. (My youngest daughter, who was 12 years old at the time, had also suffered from a fear of being sick and would only eat certain foods. She was later also diagnosed with Asperger syndrome after a long battle.) Also, I began to neglect my personal hygiene, often wearing the same clothes for days without washing.

My husband was becoming increasingly concerned, but when he tried to discuss the situation with me, I refused to listen. He kept suggesting I go back on my medication, until I accused him of just wanting me to be 'drugged up' and like a zombie.

It was only when the health visitor made a visit to complete a health check for Harry that I finally agreed that I needed help. She was extremely concerned about the state of my mental health. She had completed the Edinburgh Post Natal Depression Questionnaire with me and even though I had tried to not be completely truthful so that I would pass by scoring a low mark, I had actually scored extremely high and was presenting with severe depression. She made an urgent appointment for me to see the doctor later that day.

I tried to argue with the doctor that I was fine and I really didn't need to take medication. Lots of other people coped with life without any medication so I could do the same. The doctor looked at me and asked me why I had agreed to take insulin for diabetes when I was pregnant. I replied that it was because I needed it to stay well. There was a pause and then he said, 'So this is just the same thing. You need to take antidepressants to stay mentally well.' When he put it like that, it made sense. What had I been thinking? Of course I wasn't mentally well — that much was obvious to anyone — but I had got so entrenched in thinking that taking antidepressant medication was weak that I had lost sight of the fact that it was just like taking insulin. My body needed it. I obviously have a chemical imbalance that needs medication to balance it. I took my prescription and have been taking a 10mg maintenance dose of medication ever since. I also asked for counselling and I was referred for Cognitive Behaviour Therapy (CBT). I found CBT really helpful but, as with many interventions, it doesn't work for everyone.

When I became pregnant with my first and only child after my diagnosis of Asperger syndrome I was certain that the diagnosis would make my experience of pregnancy better. I would understand myself better and the medical staff dealing with me would also understand me better. I wouldn't be treated as an overanxious panicker; I would be understood and supported. This was not the case, unfortunately. Having the Asperger syndrome diagnosis only helped me to be kinder to myself. It helped me understand why I found some things difficult and confusing. It made no difference to any medical practitioner that I came into contact with. That is why I have written this open and honest book. Awareness of autism is vital for everyone. Until we have that awareness of difference and offer individualised care, women such as me will still have difficult experiences.

Writing this book has been similar to a labour. There have been times when I have been manic and full of energy and other times when I thought I couldn't go on. But I persevered because I am passionate about autism and pregnancy and informed choice. It is so important to raise awareness about autism and the gender differences, and to validate women's experiences. I hope this book will welcome women and girls into their tribe, where they can feel valued, strong and not judged.

Chapter 9

WHAT LIES AHEAD... ADVENTURES OF AN ASPIE DOULA

So where am I now in my journey? I am in a good place, I think. I have recently managed to complete an Advanced Certificate in Autism and I plan to complete further academic study in the future. My children are settled and, more importantly, they are happy and healthy. I am active within the autism community and hope my work with girls on the spectrum will continue to benefit girls so they don't have the negative experiences I have had. My focus has been on pregnancy and birth for over 20 years. This is why my decision to train as a doula has been almost a natural progression. I can combine my autism experience with my pregnancy and birth experience.

One of the things that I wanted to raise awareness about was the condition that I believe affected my ability to successfully breastfeed my babies. During my doula training a lot of time was spent on reflection of our own labour, birth and feeding choices. I discussed my consistent inability to breastfeed and how much this had made me feel like a failure. I realised that I had been harbouring a lot of negative emotions and grief about my breastfeeding experiences. This came out during the training. The inspirational doula delivering the training course asked me some questions about the changes my breasts had gone through during and after pregnancy and I had to confess that, thinking about it, I didn't actually experience a great deal of breast change during pregnancy or after. She suggested that I investigate a condition called breast hypoplasia.

Breast hypoplasia is also known as insufficient glandular tissue (IGT). This is a condition where the breasts do not finish forming during puberty. Breast size is not an indicator – the condition can affect small or large breasts – as it is about the glandular tissue growth within the breast. One of the traits of hypoplasia can be a lack of breast change during pregnancy. I knew I had not really experienced breast changes in the way most literature describes them. I had hoped that my breasts would increase in size during pregnancy and I used to joke with my husband that I must be the only woman whose breasts hadn't got bigger. Having completed some research into IGT, I am now certain that I have this condition. It makes complete sense because I never felt as though I had 'proper' breasts. I didn't think they looked like 'real women's' breasts. Another indicator of IGT is a large space between the breasts, and a tubular shape to them. I completely identified with that.

I went skipping back to my next session of doula training and announced that I had IGT. It was such a relief to realise that it wasn't anything that I had done wrong that meant I hadn't been able to breastfeed. Rather, it was a difference in my development – well, it wasn't the only difference I had –

so I embraced it and acknowledged it. This is something that I had always struggled to talk about because as a society we have such a sexualised attitude towards breasts that we forget that their primary function is to feed our babies. The media project an image to impressionable young girls that breasts are for sex, and if they don't look like the photoshopped versions in the underwear billboards, then there is something wrong with them. That is why I knew that I had to include this information in the book because there will be other women out there with the same condition. I had given birth to six babies and had never heard of IGT.

Breasts have always been slightly problematic for me. I've never liked wearing bras but have experimented with all sorts to make me look more womanly. They have caused me lots of discomfort over the years but I have persevered because, as I said, the media dictate that's how normal women are supposed to look. At this point in my life, if I can get away with not wearing a bra, then I don't wear one. If I have to wear a bra for modesty reasons, then I wear a sports bra, which is much more comfortable.

I only recently had my breasts measured and it turned out that I was wearing bras that were three sizes too big for me. The lady carrying out the measuring was really kind, but before I let her anywhere near me with her tape, I told her that I was on the autistic spectrum and had sensory difficulties. She visibly took a step back from me, at which I blurted out, 'It's ok, I don't bite.' She laughed nervously but I think that broke the ice. She was excellent once she knew. She brought me bras in the size I was measuring at and bras in the size I was wearing. I did buy some bras in my correct size that were padded and push-up and gave me a cleavage (I was seduced by the photoshopped pictures in the lingerie department). Those painful contraptions are now confined to the back of the drawer, gathering dust, and only come out if I have to attend a social function. They are also usually removed in the car on the way home after an event because I've already had enough discomfort for one night experiencing a social occasion, let alone a bra.

HELPFUL HINTS

Some women can have quite noticeable breast changes during pregnancy – for example, darkening of the areolas (which I had), breast tenderness and fullness. If you are tactile defensive, this can be even more uncomfortable. So go with comfort over fashion. Don't try cramming your boobs into an uncomfortable underwired torture device; pull on a sports bra instead.

What lessons have I learned from my varied pregnancies and labours? Well, as I have already indicated, while I was carrying out my doula training I had to spend a lot of time reflecting on my own labour and birth stories. It was during this period that I found myself gravitating towards natural birth. In fact, it was during the course of the training where I spent two weekends with a tribe of wonderful women that I reconnected with my true self. Actually, maybe I didn't reconnect; maybe I found my true self for the first time. I connected with my inner self and connected with my spirituality in a very strong way. As I contemplated my previous births, I thought about this image of being supported by wise women in a natural environment. This was not something I had ever thought about during my pregnancies. I maybe toyed with the idea of what I thought was natural birth with my third son, because natural birth in the 90s in suburbia was synonymous with using a birthing pool!

The setting for all of my births was in hospital. This is because my mum had me in hospital and all of the television programmes that I watched showed women going into hospital, lying on their backs and producing a neat, clean baby at the end. This was my idea of labour and birth. This was reinforced during my first marriage because my then husband didn't want to be involved in anything natural and what he perceived to be 'abnormal'. It was always important to fit in – this had been the script for my life and I certainly wasn't going to attempt to stand out in any way. My first husband's feeling was go into hospital, get the baby out by whichever is the fastest method, and job done! Of course, when you have had most of your children in this way, it becomes familiar, and familiar is safe...until you reflect on it, that is.

During my doula training I began to see that birth is a natural process. It should not automatically be a hospital procedure. There is, of course, a place for hospital intervention and treatment but I don't feel that this should be the automatic first choice. This may be even more relevant for women on the autism spectrum who, like me, may have a dislike of hospitals or who may have sensory sensitivities that become heightened during labour and birth.

Looking back at my own children's births, the two that were the fastest and most straightforward were my second and fourth births. With my second birth, even though I had pre-eclampsia, I had spent most of my early labour at home…well, actually, at a funeral and a wake the day before (with hindsight I am certain that I was in the early stage of labour while I was there). Initially, I didn't have the unhelpful presence of my first husband at my second birth, but I did have the positive presence of my mum and it was a very relaxed labour. With my fourth child, my first daughter, I laboured on my own in a side room, and although I had the help of the prostaglandin pessaries, I think a lot of the speed of the labour was down to my psychological state. I felt like a warrior mother and able to get into my own zone and roar my baby out.

Again, this highlights the importance of who is present at labour and birth. I always felt self-conscious around my first husband and he had a tendency to intimidate me. Therefore, it stands to reason that I would feel uncomfortable with him being present at the birth. I am not of the opinion that men should not be there during labour or birth but I think it shouldn't be an expectation. If a woman has a strong and trusting relationship with someone else, such as a best friend, sister, mother or doula, then I think that can really help. In the UK one of the biggest barriers is an inconsistent caregiver. It's important for all women who are going through labour and birth to have someone they trust with them. If you attend hospital and meet many different medical staff, this can be a big problem. It certainly was for me. This could be where a doula comes in – not to take the place of a medical professional, but to be a constant, trusted support. Ultimately, pregnancy, labour and birth should all be down to personal choice and women shouldn't feel that their partner has to accompany them into the labour room if they don't want them to. Indeed, men often find it extremely hard to see their partner in pain and they may not want to be present for the whole of the labour. Again, their choices should be respected and they should also have the right to move freely in and out of the room if the mother has another support person.

To recap, it can be hard to know when the beginning of labour is the real deal and when it's those pesky Braxton Hicks. The literature about the start of labour and the early signs makes it all sound so straightforward. For some women it is, and for others it may not be. I feel fairly qualified to talk about this, considering not one of my six labours started in the same way. Maybe the uncertainty around early labour is partly to do with the psychological effect of the unreliable due date. With my first pregnancy I sat and waited on my due date (as predicted by the hospital scanning machine so it must be right). I didn't want to leave the house in case 'IT' happened. (My addiction to soap operas led me to believe that there would be a massive gush of water, followed by lots of screaming and a couple of pushes, and then within a few hours it would all be over.) So I sat, I waited, I even checked my underwear regularly to see if there was a 'plug of bloody mucus' there. Nope, nothing happening.

So what should you do? Well what you shouldn't do is sit and wait. Or frenziedly check your underwear only to feel disappointed when you have a no show. You go about your usual business and try to remain busy and distracted. Otherwise, you end up climbing the walls with impatience like I did with my first child. He was due on 7 March and by the end of that day I was extremely frustrated and panicky. I ended up going into hospital way too early at 3cm dilated.

Once I got into hospital, any pains I was having promptly stopped. I think this was due to hospital phobia. Had I been less anxious, perhaps I would have stayed at home and wouldn't have had such a long and awful first birth.

As I described earlier, nothing prepared me for the feeling of bewilderment and shock after I had my first child. I had completely panicked during labour and birth and it was a traumatic experience in every way. Needless to say, when I was pregnant with my second child, I was terrified. This time, though, because I worked up until I was 37 weeks pregnant, I didn't really have the same amount of time on my hands. Once I stopped work, I had to prepare for the baby and look after a toddler. Then at week 39 the pre-eclampsia appeared and so again it was a different situation as I was taken into hospital. This time, though, I was encouraged to use different positions for labour. With my first labour I was on a foetal heart monitor and then had an epidural so I was on my back in bed for most of my labour. The second time I was encouraged to get onto all fours and lean over the bed. This is much more comfortable as you are working with gravity. Not rocket science really, is it?!

I decided with my third child that I would have a water birth. This was a relatively new concept in the hospital where I was giving birth and was encouraged mainly as a means of pain relief. I love water. It soothes me so much that the idea of using it as pain relief really appealed to me. This should have been a straightforward labour, considering my second one, but I fell foul of the watch-and-wait technique instead of the keep-busy-and-distract technique.

The points that really stick out for me in my own labours are what my head was saying. So many psychological factors can have a negative influence on labour: For example, the 'white coat effect', which means that as soon as you approach a hospital your legs want to run in the opposite direction and take you far away. Another one is the 'unsupportive birth partner effect' (no explanation necessary). And how about the 'I'm-not-ready-to-be-a-mother effect'. The mind is a powerful thing and can affect the body in many ways.

Active labour or 'soap opera' labour? Would you like support from a trusted birth companion? It's your choice. When I talk about active labour versus soap opera labour, I think of it this way: in soaps and television dramas, birth is portrayed as being either clinical or dramatic. For example, the birth which shows a woman being pushed into a room in a wheelchair (that is, not walking and therefore not active in early labour). Then the next time you see her, straight after giving birth, she is sitting up in bed with full make-up, perfect hair, a big smile and a clean baby that resembles a cherub nestled in her arms. Not too realistic really. Alternatively, there is the big drama where a woman collapses in pain and within minutes is screaming – again on her back on the bed in hospital – and pushing. Even then, she manages to retain full make-up. Now for someone like me who grew up observing and copying others, this has a certain influence. So it's important to have an open mind and understand that labour and birth also operates on a spectrum from fast, textbook births to dramatic, emergency births. Not to mention everything in between.

The challenges of labour and birth for a woman on the autism spectrum are the same as for any woman, but they are magnified. There is also the difficulty around understanding language and expressive language. When you are in a state of heightened anxiety, it becomes difficult to process instructions and the choices being offered to you. A perfect example of this breakdown was when I was asked to move rooms with my last birth. It also becomes hard to verbalise your needs if you are in pain or scared. In the Appendices there are some trimester, labour and birth 'Top Tips' for mums-to-be to use to empower themselves. There are tips for dads-to-be as well, detailing how they can help their partner through all stages of pregnancy and labour. There are suggestions on things that are common in pregnancy and things that you may want to discuss with your obstetric practitioner. I have also included some thoughts on how to handle the social demands following your baby's birth, useful birth positions and ideas for an autism friendly hospital bag. Additionally, Appendix 10 includes some advice for professionals, who may be reading this book, on how to support a woman on the spectrum. If you are an expectant mum or dad you may want to share the advice for professionals with whoever is your caregiver. There is also a template to help you to complete your birth wishes (plan) and a flow chart to give you an idea of how a typical labour and birth would progress.

First Trimester Top Tips

Weeks 10–12

- *Morning sickness:* This doesn't just happen in the morning – it can last all day; and it's not always vomiting – sometimes it's just an overwhelming nausea. This may be more intense for women on the spectrum due to sensory sensitivities.

  ○ *Top tips for mums-to-be:* I tried bands for sea sickness in one pregnancy and they helped. I also ate ginger biscuits. I tried crystallised ginger but personally I found this too strong and it made me feel worse. Try to eat little and often throughout the day.

  ○ *Top tips for dads-to-be:* Be sensitive to the fact that morning sickness does not only happen in the morning but can last all day. Keep the supply of ginger biscuits topped up and bring your partner a small snack before she gets up in the morning.

- *Frequency of urination*: This can mean racing around trying to find a toilet, then peeing less than a teaspoonful. Some women on the autism spectrum are hypersensitive to bladder changes (like me). I constantly felt the need to go to the toilet in the first trimester.

  ○ *Top tips for mums-to-be*: Drink plenty of fluids, preferably water or juice. Since I don't drink water, I drank lots of squash and herbal tea. Discuss having to pee a lot with your healthcare professional as it may be a sign of a urine infection.

  ○ *Top tips for dads-to-be*: Be prepared to make regular toilet stops. Try not to say, 'Surely you don't need to go again.'

- *Feeling exhausted*: Many people with autism feel tired and suffer with social exhaustion. This increases during pregnancy as your baby is growing rapidly and using up a lot of your energy.

  ○ *Top tips for mums-to-be*: Try to cut down on your workload and have naps when you can. And do *not* feel guilty. As women on the spectrum, we are prone to being perfectionists. I worked full-time during my second pregnancy and missed out on time with my toddler because I was so exhausted that I would just crawl into bed when I got home. With my last pregnancy my manager was already making reasonable adjustments for my Asperger's and she also encouraged me to adapt my working hours. Try to do the same. Going for a nap can provide a good excuse to avoid social situations.

○ *Top tips for dads-to-be*: Understand that your partner may be constantly exhausted. Tell her she is beautiful even if she falls asleep with her mouth open and dribbling.

• *Tender breasts*: Many women on the autism spectrum have sensory difficulties with clothing – bras in particular. This can lead to a lot of discomfort during pregnancy.

○ *Top tips for mums-to-be*: Try wearing a sports bra (I have to confess to wearing these all the time now as they're so comfortable). You may also find that placing a warm or cool damp flannel over your breasts eases discomfort.

○ *Top tips for dads-to-be*: Remember that in pregnancy breasts can be painful. Very painful.

• *Feeling faint*: This is something that has affected me since childhood, and it got worse during pregnancy. In pregnancy the extra demand on your body's blood system can make you dizzy. In my case, if I felt dizzy, I would panic and this increased the dizziness – a vicious cycle.

○ *Top tips for mums-to-be*: Don't panic. Keep your breathing deep and slow, and sit down until the feeling passes. Avoid standing for long periods and never take hot baths. Accept that dizzy or fainting spells may happen and that this is quite common in pregnancy. However, it's important that you tell your doctor or midwife so they can check you out.

○ *Top tips for dads-to-be*: Remind your partner to eat 'little and often' to keep their blood sugars balanced. Support them in keeping healthy snacks in their bag such as, bananas, raisins, dried apricots etc. Also remind the mum-to-be to keep hydrated and as their partner remember to keep snacks and bottles of water with you, in the car or in a lunch bag. Encourage your partner to lie on their side after 16 weeks of pregnancy to relieve pressure from the weight of the uterus.

• *Changing shape*: By the end of this first trimester your bump may be slightly visible. This was the part I was dreading. Having always been very skinny, I was worried about how I would feel about no longer having a neat shape. However, when my bump started to appear, I was thrilled and couldn't wait to get bigger.

○ *Top tips for mums-to-be*: Don't obsess about your weight. If this is something you already have an issue with, explain to your medical practitioner that you have autism and that body image or weight control is something you need support with.

○ *Top tips for dads-to-be*: Reassure her that her changing shape is beautiful, and remind her of the end goal: your beautiful baby.

- *Mood swings:* You may experience tears one minute, joy the next. This is so difficult to deal with, in my opinion, because women on the autism spectrum often have difficulties managing their emotions. We are overly sensitive to other people's moods, especially if they are negative. When pregnancy hormones kick in, this can magnify the sensitivities. Some days I would burst into tears if I heard a sad song, and other days I was like something from the *Exorcist.*

  - *Top tips for mums-to-be:* Try and get plenty of rest, as being tired will impact on your mood. Try a little light exercise too, a gentle swim or some antenatal yoga may help to distress you. Take a support person with you or explain to the person running the class about how your autism affects you in new situations. Do some positive self-talk! Don't feel guilty if you feel irritable or moody; remind yourself that hormones are to blame. Talk to someone you trust. If you have an understanding GP, counsellor, autism support person then discuss how you feel with them.

  - *Top tips for dads-to-be:* If she bursts into tears at a nappy advert, don't ask her what is wrong. Just use comforting words or a comforting touch. If she turns into a raging inferno because you left the toilet seat up, don't take it personally. Hormones in pregnancy are complicated and unpredictable. Hormones in a pregnant woman on the spectrum can be double the trouble.

Important note: I want to tell people that the idea that people on the spectrum (male or female) are lacking in empathy is complete rubbish. Most people on the spectrum feel empathy; they just have difficulties in putting themselves in other people's shoes. This is definitely a skill that can be picked up over a period of time.

Second Trimester Top Tips

Weeks 13–28

- *Decide whether you want to find out the sex of your baby at your 20-week scan:* Think of the pros and cons of your decision. I desperately wanted to know all of my babies' genders but this was only actually offered for my fifth and sixth pregnancies. I have never liked the idea of surprises and I felt no different when wanting to find out whether I was expecting a girl or a boy. I needed to know what to prepare for, but obviously it's a personal decision.

- *Choose your birth partner.* I have written a lot about points to consider when choosing a birth partner and it is important to consider your options: partner, sister, friend or doula. You may want to have more than one birth partner, but if you plan to give birth in hospital you will need to discuss how many people are allowed to attend your birth.

- *Stay active*: Try to stay active by taking up swimming or yoga. Remember, you may be more comfortable having a support person with you. It is also a good idea to find out when your local pool is at its quietest in order to minimise social difficulties and sensory overload.

- *Buy maternity clothes (including bras)*: Now may be the time to choose a maternity wardrobe. You may not want to spend a lot of money on clothes, so think about acquiring a few key items that will see you through. Give consideration to clothing material as you may experience more hypersensitivity when pregnant.

- *Get some sleep*: I often tell people that I haven't had a good night's sleep for 25 years. When you're pregnant and have sensory sensitivity, investing in extra pillows, back wedges and different textured bedding may help. I had a V-shaped pillow, three normal pillows and a long pillow wedged around me with my last pregnancy. The long pillow rested between my legs and supported my bump, and the V-shaped pillow supported my neck. I also had to buy a different long pillow because the first one was made of polyester, which irritated me.

- *Bond with your baby*: Babies can hear sounds from about 23 weeks, so talking and singing to your baby can develop your bond. If you feel self-conscious talking directly to your bump or singing to it, then read your favourite book or magazine out loud.

- *Use a foetal Doppler*: This is a good way to listen in to your baby and ease your anxiety. Dopplers can be hired for a one-off deposit and a monthly fee, or you can pay in a single instalment.

- *Start to tell people*: The second trimester may well be when you begin to tell people about your pregnancy (although they may have guessed from your constant trips to the loo and your habit of falling asleep mid-conversation!).

- *Consider your changing body*: Accepting these changes will affect every woman differently. If you identify with my experiences, that may be helpful but there will also be women reading this book who don't identify and that's ok too. Some of the body changes you may experience are listed below.

  ○ *Breast changes*: You may experience some breast leaks at this stage. Don't worry – there are not gallons of breast milk about to gush out. The leakage is colostrum, which is the first milk your baby will get from you, and it's a sign that your body is preparing to feed your baby. (Not everyone experiences this leakage and if this is the case for you it doesn't mean you will have any breastfeeding problems.) Use breast pads but remember to try out free samples, if possible, to make sure that they feel comfortable.

  ○ *Leg cramps*: Leg cramps can become quite common during the second trimester. This may be due to the extra weight that you are carrying. Often these cramps can happen at night and you may also suffer with restless leg symptoms. Restless leg symptoms are when you need to keep moving your legs at night when you are trying to sleep. This can be to alleviate tingling or burning in your legs. Avoid standing or sitting with your legs crossed for long periods of time. Stretch your calf muscles regularly during the day and several times before you go to bed. Also rotate your ankles and wiggle your toes regularly throughout the day. Wear comfortable shoes with plenty of support. Try and take a short, gentle walk every day. Check with your medical practitioner before embarking on a new exercise. Try taking a warm bath before bed to relax your muscles.

○ *Constipation*: Pregnancy hormones cause your bowels to slow down, so try to eat food that is high in fibre and drink plenty of water.

○ *Heartburn (indigestion)*: This occurs in pregnancy due to the placenta producing a lot of the hormone progesterone. This relaxes the valve that separates the oesophagus from the stomach. This can be worse when you're lying down as the gastric acid can travel back up the pipe. This causes the burning sensation which is heartburn. For lots of women the problem doesn't begin until later in pregnancy. It may also become worse towards the end of the pregnancy when your growing uterus starts to push up on your stomach. The discomfort may range from slightly uncomfortable to intense and frequent. Try to eat little and often instead of having big meals. I am a grazer anyway, but even that didn't stop the heartburn, so I tried drinking milk. This acts as an antacid but eventually I had to move on to the hard stuff: heartburn medication as prescribed by a doctor.

○ *Stretch marks*: There is nothing you can do to prevent stretch marks. Genetics play a large role in this so if your mother or sister had them, you're more likely to get them. There is no evidence that lotions and creams actually work in reducing stretch marks but there is no harm in using a moisturiser on your expanding tummy. (There are some nice, light moisturisers on the market that don't leave you feeling sticky, which is a sensory issue of mine).

• *Antenatal appointments*: During the second trimester you will probably attend your antenatal booking appointment. Depending on where you live, you may also be offered an initial appointment before your booking appointment. The booking appointment will be a long one, and if you would feel more comfortable having this take place at home, it is worth requesting this.

During this appointment you will be asked about your lifestyle and health and, if applicable, any past pregnancies.

This is also an opportunity to clarify whether your midwife or obstetrician is aware that you have been diagnosed as being on the autism spectrum. It is important to discuss how your autism impacts on you and how this could potentially affect you in your pregnancy, labour and birth.

You will be offered some screening tests and will be given information about the anomaly scan. This scan will usually be offered between 18 and 20 weeks and will check your baby's growth. By the time of your 20-week scan it should be easy to tell the sex of the baby.

After your initial appointment you will be asked to attend further antenatal appointments. Where these take place will depend on where you live and if you are healthy and expected to have a straightforward pregnancy and birth.

You may want to look into antenatal classes. If you know that you will find it difficult to attend classes, can a partner or friend go with you? Or you might consider hiring a doula. Alternatively, some websites offer online antenatal classes that you can watch from the comfort of your own home.

All in all, the second trimester is supposed to be the best, the one where most of the initial flooding of pregnancy hormones subsides slightly and you feel calm and beautiful. That's what the books say. In reality, some women feel like that, which is great, but many others will still feel plagued with nausea, anxiety and other feelings. In fact, it's very common. Don't beat yourself up because your experience is not the same as what the literature says it should be. Pregnancy is different for everyone and for women on the spectrum many of those changes feel very intense and strange. I was often advised to use affirmations: for example, to look at myself in the mirror and say out loud, 'You're amazing' and other positive exclamations. I found this hard to do, so I adapted this for myself by saying, 'You're ok.' Being ok is enough.

Third Trimester Top Tips

Weeks 29–40 plus

- *Baby movements:* You may find that these slow down a little now as your baby gets bigger and has less room to move around. By now you will probably recognise the patterns of your baby's movements. If you experience less movement than is usual for your baby, contact your midwife. I was in and out of hospital with most of my pregnancies due to concerns over my babies' movements and it was never a problem to have my babies monitored.

- *Pre-eclampsia:* This struck me during my second pregnancy and is a potential complication you need to be aware of. It can occur from 20 weeks of pregnancy but is more common in the third trimester. The antenatal tests carried out by your midwife look for any indications of pre-eclampsia, such as high blood pressure and protein in your urine. However, sometimes pre-eclampsia comes on even though the tests give no indication of it. That's what happened to me. I had normal blood pressure throughout all of my pregnancies and no protein in my urine during my second pregnancy, which is when I developed pre-eclampsia. I woke up one morning with a severe headache and I couldn't lift my head off the pillow. My vision was blurred and my fingers and feet were swollen, as was my face. My GP came out to see me and said I needed to go to hospital immediately. When I got there it was discovered that I was already in early labour and my son was born later that night.

- *Braxton Hicks*: These mild, irregular tightenings prepare your uterus for labour. Although they are present throughout pregnancy, most women only notice them from around week 25 and they usually only become frequent and intense in the third trimester. Notice how they feel and how often you experience them. Use them as a time to practise your breathing.

- *Breast changes*: During the last trimester you may find that your breasts begin to leak a little. This can be a bit of a sensory challenge. I found that using breast pads in my sports bra helped. I had to get over the barrier in my mind that breast pads were not to be worn until I had given birth! Once I had managed that, it helped to stop me feeling uncomfortable. I also had to try lots of different types of pad. It's a bit like finding the right sanitary towel – you many need to try several different brands and designs until you find one or two you're comfortable with. (I say 'one or two' just in case the manufacturer inconsiderately decides to change the way they are made. This happened to me – in my opinion there was nothing wrong with the pads but it was felt 'improvement' was needed.)

- *Birth wishes or birth plan*: In the 80s birth plans were high on the agenda. Now they often appear to be something that hospitals just pay lip service to. Instead of talking about a 'plan' I prefer to call this my 'birth wishes'. You can find a sample in Appendix 6.

- *Hospital bag*: if you are having your baby in a hospital or at a birthing centre, you will need to think about what to pack. You will find suggestions in Appendices 7–9.

- *Visit the place where you will be giving birth*: If this is a hospital, you can usually go on a tour of the labour and birth suite. Even though I had given birth at the same hospital four times previously, I decided to take a tour before my fifth child was born. I'm glad I did because the tour included the operating theatre and this was where I ended up having my emergency C-section. Having been there before made it seem slightly less daunting when I ended up in there for delivery. If you are on the autism spectrum, pre-tutoring about new places is quite often highly recommended. In this age of the Internet you can also check out the hospital or birth centre's website. It is important to remember that you have a choice when giving birth. Know your options and make sure that you are happy with them. This is the place where you will meet your little miracle for the first time. It is important to feel empowered to have the environment that you feel comfortable with.

- *Aches and pains*: This trimester can see an increase in backache and joint pains. Above all, try not to lift heavy things. Now may be the time to have your partner practise massage on you using aromatherapy oils in preparation for labour and birth. If you experience real discomfort then, discuss this with your medical practitioner who can advise you on support aids.

- *Make practical arrangements for the birth*: For example, do you know how long it is from home to the place where you will give birth? If you have other children, have you got someone lined up to take care of them? If you're having a home birth make sure you have everything you need, especially if you're hiring a pool (make sure you have this set up in advance and have checked how long it takes to fill).

- *Feeding your baby*: I would recommend reading up on feeding your baby. From my own experience I would suggest that it is better to be prepared and have gained information during pregnancy rather than wait until you have given birth.

- *Social media*: When I had my older children, I felt very isolated. As unbelievable as it seems now, in the old days before the Internet (yes, there was a time before the Internet!) people had to connect socially by going out and joining groups. All very social. As you have read, I found that really hard to do.

In my last pregnancy, even though I had my diagnosis, I still didn't get any help. I also found it difficult to disclose my diagnosis. I think that is mainly because I am articulate and can act quite well in social situations. For example, when I give conference talks or deliver training, I often have people come up to me and say, 'But you look so normal.' My reply to that is, 'Oh no, I tried really hard today to not look normal.' On a serious note. I do tell people that this is my 'mask'. They wouldn't want to see me when I'm having a meltdown, which I do frequently. They don't know how socially exhausted I get just being around them. Autism is a hidden disability but that doesn't make it a lesser disability. It makes it harder to get support. I have a good friend who comes to events with me and, without either of us realising it, she has become my carer/support person – call it what you will.

The advent of social media was therefore extremely helpful in my last pregnancy. I could research all my questions and concerns on the Internet, I could subscribe to pregnancy and baby websites and I could communicate with other pregnant mums, all without having to suffer the crippling anxiety of verbally interacting with people. This helped me enormously. There are many good websites out there for pregnant and new mums, so take a look.

Labour and Birth Top Tips

There are three stages of labour.

1. The first stage is when your contractions start and begin to gradually open up your cervix. The first stage consists of *early labour, active labour* and *transition* (see Appendix 12).

2. The second stage is when you push your baby out.

3. The third stage is when you deliver the placenta.

First stage of labour

In the first stage of labour you may experience all or some of the following:

*   Continuing lower back pain or abdominal pain.

*   Painful contractions (tightening of the uterus) that occur at regular intervals and get closer together as labour progresses.

- A gush (or trickle) of amniotic fluid. If this happens, call your maternity unit as once your waters break there is a risk of infection.

- A blood-tinged or brown, jelly-like mucus plug. This is also known as a 'show'. This can appear when birth is imminent or when it is still a few days away.

- Some mothers experience loose bowel movements.

When you experience the above signs, you may want to contact your labour ward if you are giving birth in hospital or your midwife if you are planning a maternity unit or home birth.

There is no specific length of time for labour and the first stage can be long and uncomfortable or relatively short. It is for you to decide when you want to leave home for the hospital or the birth centre. The usual advice if there are no problems is to stay at home as long as you can.

Second stage of labour

Provided you are not still experiencing the effects of an epidural, in the second stage of labour you are likely to experience the following feelings:

- You will probably feel the pressure of your baby's head low down in your pelvis.

- With each contraction you may have the urge to bear down and push. Be guided by your body and let it push when the urge comes. Remember to breathe.

- After a period of time you may begin to feel a stinging sensation. This is your vagina starting to stretch around your baby's head.

- Your midwife may tell you she can see the baby's head and advise you to start panting. This stops you pushing with the next contraction so that your baby is born slowly and gently.

This stage of labour can sometimes be easier than the first stage. The urge to push tells you that your baby should be with you soon, so you have a renewed purpose. I have to tell you that the urges to push are like having a poop. In fact, sometimes when you're pushing in labour, you may even pass a little poop. Don't be embarrassed – it's all in a day's work to people who work in the birth sector.

Third stage of labour

The third stage of labour begins when your baby is born and ends when you have delivered the placenta and the empty bag of waters, which is attached to it. These come away as your uterus contracts after birth. You can choose (as indicated in your birth wishes) whether to have a natural or a managed third stage. I had no idea that these options were available with my four vaginal births, so make sure you have all the information you need for an informed choice.

Let's Talk about Labour and Birth Positions

I spent most of my pre-pregnant life thinking that there was only one position in which to give birth – on your back – which is the position I adopted in my first labour. Imagine my surprise when the midwife in my second labour asked me which position I wanted – yes, '*wanted*', to give birth in. I have to confess I thought she was joking. I obviously looked very confused, so she tried to help me along. Would I like to squat? 'Erm...no thanks.' Would I like to try all fours? 'Absolutely not.' Would I like to stand up? 'What, and have the baby drop on its head?! Definitely not. Just put me on my back where I'm supposed to be and stop trying to confuse me.' After some persuasion, I did try some of those positions, and even though I still went back to my default position of being on my back for birth, I found a lot of comfort in the other positions while I was labouring. So that you don't experience the same surprise as I did, let's have a look at some labour and birth positions.

Labour (first stage) positions

- Lean on a chair, a birth partner or a work surface if you're still at home.

- Put your arms around your birth partner's neck and lean on them. If you have difficulties with proximity to people, this may be heightened when you're in pain so discuss that with your birth partner before you go into labour. You may not be able to tolerate any kind of touch when you're in pain. You can always lean on the bed with your partner nearby.

- Sit on a birthing ball. Some hospitals provide them, but if you have found comfort using one in pregnancy and you definitely want to use one for labour, it may be a good idea to take your own. You may prefer its sameness and familiarity, and no hospital should have a problem with you providing some self-comfort.

- Sit astride a chair facing the back, with a pillow for support.

- Go on to all fours.

- Sit on the toilet. If you're worried about the baby suddenly dropping into the toilet bowl (and this is something that some women are terrified of), sit on the toilet with the lid down and a towel across for comfort.

APPENDIX 5 LET'S TALK ABOUT LABOUR AND BIRTH POSITIONS

Birth (second stage) positions

- On all fours (on your hands and knees).

- In a squatting position.

- In a semi-sitting position.

- Lying on your side in a semi-upright position.

- Leaning forward in a supported standing position.

Try to keep as active as you can and change positions if you become uncomfortable. Try to avoid the 'soap opera' on-your-back birth position if you can. Obviously, if you have an epidural, you have to stay in bed as you will be numb from the waist down. Still, try not to lie flat on your back as it can reduce the baby's oxygen supply. Your midwife will help you to get into a comfortable position on the bed – usually in a sideways position or semi-reclining, using pillows.

You can discuss birth and labour positions with your midwife or doula and practise during pregnancy whatever feels comfortable for you.

LABOUR AND BIRTH CRIB SHEET FOR DADS-TO-BE

- Be aware of your partner's birth wishes. Talk them through with her and know what she wants so that you can advocate for her if required.

- Consider hiring a doula if you feel that you both may need support during labour.

- Be aware of sensory sensitivities and have a bag of resources ready if needed.

- Sometimes sensory sensitivities can change. For example, if your partner usually can only tolerate light touch this may change in labour. Be guided by her.

- Do your best to keep anxieties down to a minimum.

- If your partner wants someone else present during labour and birth, try not to take it personally.

- Understand that this is you and your partner's experience of giving birth. If you need to discuss in private an intervention that is offered, ask everyone else to leave the room.

- If you feel that your partner is becoming overwhelmed, you can ask everyone to leave the room until she has regained her equilibrium.

- Agree in advance a means for your partner to indicate that she is becoming overwhelmed. This could be a password or a gesture. If this is used, it's time to clear out of the room for a while.

- Remember to eat and drink – you need to look after yourself as well.

- When the baby is born, you too can have skin-to-skin contact with them. This can also be a good idea if your partner is overwhelmed or still in sensory overload.

Birth Wishes (Birth Plan)

You can write your birth wishes however you want to. You can use colored ink, little pictures...whatever you want. This is your birth and your wishes for that birth. Include a Plan B just in case things change during your labour. You can even use a flow chart if that would be helpful.

Here are some suggestions of what to write:

- *About you:* Indicate that you are on the autism spectrum and detail anything that you feel hospital staff need to know about how autism affects you. Include how you may want to communicate if you are in meltdown or a heightened sensory state. What sensory sensitivities do you have and how may these affect you? What can staff do to help you?

- *Birth partner:* Say who your birth partner will be. You can choose whoever you want but some hospitals have a policy regarding the number of people you can have with you, so check this out. Question any decisions you're not happy with. Your birth wishes should be personalised for you. Write down whether you want your birth supporters to be with you all through labour or whether you want them at certain stages.

- *Interventions*: Do you want any interventions to speed up your labour, such as a membrane sweep, or would you rather wait and see what happens naturally? If any medical interventions are suggested, do you and your birth partner want to be left in private to discuss them? If you need an assisted birth or a Caesarean, who do you want to stay with you, if anyone?

- *Pain relief*: Give details of how you want to manage your pain. Do you want medical pain relief? If so, is there an order you would prefer to have it in? Write down natural methods as well, such as breathing. Will you be using hypnosis or aromatherapy? Are there any key words that you want used or avoided? For example, some people prefer to have no mention of pain or any negative words during their labour.

- *Positions for labour and birth*: Which positions do you want to use in labour and which position would you prefer to birth in. Do you want to remain active for as long as possible? If you are having a water birth do you want to birth in the water or just use it for pain relief? Will you have your partner in the water with you?

- *Comfort items*: Write down any self-soothing methods you would like to use, including bean bags, a birthing ball, music, visualisation props and massage oils.

- *Monitoring your baby's heartbeat*: Do you want occasional monitoring of your baby's heartbeat with a hand-held device, or continuous monitoring which will involve being hooked up to a machine and restrict your movements?

- *Assisted birth:* If your baby needs help to be born, would you prefer forceps or ventouse?

- *Delivering the placenta and cutting the cord:* Find out what the options are and state what you feel comfortable with.

- *Holding your baby:* Do you want skin-to-skin contact? Would you like your baby to be handed to you directly after the birth or cleaned up first? Would you prefer your baby to be handed to your partner for skin-to-skin contact until you are ready?

- *Feeding your baby:* Will you be breastfeeding or formula feeding? If you are breastfeeding, make sure you make it clear whether you want your baby to be exclusively breastfed.

- *Unexpected situations:* What would you like to happen if your baby needs to go to the special care baby unit?

My Hospital Bag: What to Pack for Labour

- *Your birth wishes.*

- *Your maternity notes.*

- *Comfortable nightdress:* Choose one that preserves your dignity if you are walking around during active labour.

- *A dressing gown:* Choose one that opens easily for breastfeeding and skin-to-skin contact but that is long enough for modesty. Hospitals are usually kept warm, so a lightweight one may be the most suitable. Try to take dark-coloured nighties and dressing gowns in case of leakages.

- *Slippers:* Bring ones that are easy to get on and off as it's hard to bend down after giving birth, especially if you have a C-section.

- *Socks:* Feet can get cold in labour, especially just before birth.

- *A one-litre bottle of water or ready-diluted squash.*

- *Snacks:* These will maintain your energy levels. (It's important to bring these from home if there is a particular brand you like as you may not be able to get the same one in the hospital shop.)

- *Hand-held fan.*

- *Massage oil or lotion.*

- *Tissues scented with your favourite calming fragrance.*

- *Lip balm:* Lips can become dry in hospital.

- *Water spray:* This will help you to cool down.

- *Birthing ball:* Alternatively, check whether the hospital or birthing centre already has one that will be available for you to use.

- *Birthing soundtrack.*

- *Your own pillows:* If you're in hospital, these will be a reminder of home.

- *Bendy straws:* These will help you to drink when you're in labour.

- *Photo or picture that you can use to help you visualise:* This can be of a safe or favourite place, or a person, or your special interest.

- *Anything you usually use to self-soothe:* For example, earplugs, headphones, fidget toys, bean bags, etc.

- *Camera.*

- *Money.*

- *Mobile.*

- *Sleepsuit for baby.*

My Hospital Bag: What to Pack for My Postnatal Stay

- *A going-home outfit:* Remember that you won't be back to your pre-pregnancy size immediately. Don't make the mistake of taking in clothes that fitted you nine months previously (I'm talking from experience). With my first baby I brought leggings to go home in that had fitted my six-stone self. I had gone up to twelve stone during pregnancy and my baby didn't weigh six stone at birth. I didn't think of that. My leggings only reached my knees...

- *Nursing bras:* Pack two or three.

- *Breast pads:* Make sure you have tried out different brands for comfort.

- *Maternity pads:* You will need a couple of packs.

- *Nightdress:* Take a comfortable one that is front opening if you are planning to breastfeed. I bought three of the same type as they were comfortable.

- *Toiletries*: I bought travel-sized empty bottles and filled them with my favourite toiletries.

- *Knickers*: Take old, stretchy knickers that you don't mind being thrown away. Big pants are useful if you have had a C-section as they reach above your scar. I bought value brand knickers from the local supermarket and they were perfect.

- *Eye mask and earplugs*: In the unfortunate event that you end up in a multi-bed ward because there is no single room available, these items could be a godsend (I wish I'd thought to take them in). I usually wear earplugs these days because my sensory sensitivity has heightened as I have got older and I don't sleep very well. They help a little but I had to try many different textures, shapes and sizes before I found some I can tolerate. Now I buy multipacks off the Internet.

- *Money*: Always useful if you want to buy something from the hospital shop.

- *Magazines, tablet computer, mobile phone and charger.*

My Hospital Bag: What to Pack for My Baby

- *Sleepsuits and vests:* Pack two or three.

- *Nappies:* Your newborn will get through approximately a dozen per day.

- *Muslin cloths:* These are the best invention ever! I only discovered them when I had my last baby and they were so useful for mopping up breast milk, baby sick, spilled drinks etc! I still use them now three years on.

- *Cotton wool, baby lotion or baby wipes:* For cleaning your baby's bottom.

- *Baby hat:* This is for taking your baby home in. Most heat is lost through the head so put one on when you leave the warm environment of the hospital. (At home and in hospital, though, a baby doesn't need to constantly wear a hat and it might cause them to overheat.)

- *Baby blanket.*

- *Scratch mitts.*

- *Snowsuit or coat:* Only necessary for winter babies.

- *Car seat:* Some hospitals have a policy whereby they won't let you leave unless your baby is in a car seat.

Advice for Medical Staff Working with Pregnant Women on the Autistic Spectrum

- *Be autism aware.* Nobody expects you to be an expert in conditions on the autism spectrum, but in the same way that you would show professional interest in caring for a person with any disability, do the same for someone living with autism.

- *Looks can be deceptive.* Autism is a hidden disability, and if you have met one person with autism that's all you have met. Everyone is an individual. (For more information, see Appendix 11.)

- *Sensory sensitivity.* Be aware that the majority of people on the autism spectrum have some kind of sensory sensitivity. This can be heightened when they are anxious, stressed or overwhelmed. You don't have to be an expert on this subject – just be mindful.

- *Communication:* Autism is a *social communication* difficulty. When an autistic person is upset or highly anxious, their ability to communicate or understand verbal communication can become very impaired.

- *It's all about the social:* Be aware that hospital can be an extremely stressful environment for a woman on the autism spectrum. If you can, offer her privacy in the form of her own room – it will make a HUGE difference to her emotional well-being.

- *Share:* You don't have to be an autism expert, but you can work with autism professionals in your area.

- *Remember that rates of diagnosis of women on the autism spectrum are rising:* You will more than likely care for more than one woman on the autism spectrum during your career.

Appendix 11

How My Autism May Look

Remember, autism is a hidden disability; but if you take a closer look, you may see the following:

- I may be highly anxious about what might seem like trivial things to you. You may see me thinking about the worst-case scenario, but what is happening is that my anxiety is increasing with each and every setback, difficulty or assault on my senses.

- I may appear highly anxious when pregnant (even if the pregnancy was planned) as a result of tocophobia (fear of pregnancy and childbirth). This may seem like an irrational fear to you and you may think I'm being ridiculous. You may tell me everything will be fine. However, this fear is not irrational to me – it's completely real and justified.

- I may appear quiet, shy and compliant, and not interested in asking questions; or I may say that everything is 'fine.' What is actually happening is that you need an answer quickly but I am taking time to process what you have said. I am also very anxious, which affects my ability to understand what you have said.

- I may need to have many sensory breaks in the form of toilet breaks, leaving the room, and not answering telephone calls, emails or texts. You may see this as me fidgeting or being ignorant. What is actually happening is that my anxiety levels are rising and affecting my senses so I need a break.

- I may often need time away from people or social situations. This may look like I'm being aloof or stand-offish but I'm actually experiencing sensory overload and need time to decompress.

- I may become deeply interested in a specific thing or topic and need to engage in it or discuss it. This could look like I'm boring or self-centred. What's actually happening is that I find safety and comfort in my special interest and need to engage in it to self-soothe.

- I may need extra time to process what you have said to me and then clarify it. You may see me as being unresponsive or pedantic. What is happening is that I have taken in a lot of verbal language and I need time to process and understand it. Then I need time to formulate a reply to you. This means that in a short space of time my brain is working overtime.

- I may be rigid in my thoughts and ideas. They may seem unimportant to you but they are very important to me. You might see it as me being spoiled or selfish. I'm not. This is part of my autism. My brain is wired differently and I only see situations in black or white, or as wrong or right.

- I may be extremely organised (colour coding my maternity notes); *or* I may not remember to bring my notes with me and, if I do, they may be dog-eared and coffee-stained. You may think I'm fussy and uptight or you may think I'm careless and exasperating. What is happening is that my executive function is playing up. Either way, I'm anxious and overwhelmed.

- I may give you too much detail about things (oversharing) or not know which bits of information are relevant, so I tell you everything. You may see this as me being self-absorbed or indiscreet. This is part of my autism. I cannot filter out the important pieces of information or know where to start or finish.

- I may not tell you important things and stick to short or one-word answers. This can be seen as meaning that everything is fine, when it may not be, or me being rude and uncooperative. What's happening is that, again, I may not see what you see as important. I may have taken your question literally and given you an answer based on that, or I may be overwhelmed and unable to engage.

- During pregnancy and labour I may suffer from a high level of pain. You may see this as me being weak and a 'drama queen'. I am actually experiencing high sensory sensitivity. I may be the opposite, however, and have a very high pain threshold.

- I may struggle in a hospital room with others. You might think I'm being precious and over-sensitive. What's actually happening is that I am experiencing high levels of social anxiety and sensory sensitivity.

- I may need prompting to hold and feed my baby. This can look as though I don't have any interest in my baby or I am neglectful. What is happening is that I may be overwhelmed from the birth and may be in shut-down mode. It may also mean that I have become distracted and may need support and help, not criticism.

- I may constantly want to hold my baby and be overly attentive to his needs. You may think I am an over-protective mother who needs to lighten up. The reality is that I am in tune with my baby and that's absolutely ok.

How Labour Progresses

First stage of labour: Onset of labour or early labour

- Mild contractions or irregular contractions.

- Lower back pain.

- 'Nesting' – the urge to tidy and clean.

- Diarrhoea.

- Excessive mucus discharge.

- Waters breaking.

- Feeling emotional.

First stage of labour: Active labour

- The long muscles in the uterus begin to contract more regularly. This will make contractions more regular, more painful and closer together. Contractions are usually approximately every 3–4 minutes but individuals differ.

- Active labour lasts until the cervix has fully dilated.

- During this time you can stay at home being as active as you want until you feel the need to go to the hospital/birthing centre and receive further pain relief.

- If you're having a home birth, just try to stay active and use whichever coping mechanisms you have chosen (such as water, music, massage etc.).

- Active labour usually lasts 4–8 hours for first-time births. However, it can be shorter or longer.

NOW IS THE TIME FOR PAIN RELIEF IF YOU HAVE CHOSEN TO HAVE ANY.

First stage of labour: Transition

- Transition usually occurs when you are 8–10cm dilated.

- It's called 'transition' because it marks the change between the first and second stages of labour.

- It can be very painful and intense, and it may feel as if there is no let-up between contractions.

- Some women feel an increase in anxiety and panic at this stage. It is important to know that this anxious feeling is completely normal.

- There may be a lot of bloody discharge and you may feel sick.

- Transition can last from minutes to hours, but the good news is it means your baby is getting close to being born.

Second stage of labour: Pushing your baby out

- Once the cervix is fully dilated (10cm), the work of pushing your baby out begins.

- In the second stage your contractions may be further apart (the rest-and-be-thankful stage), giving you time to pause and have some respite before the next push.

- Your muscles will contract, giving you the urge to bear down (similar to having a bowel movement).

- Timing of the second stage depends on the individual, and it can be a quick descent for the baby or a gradual one.

- Eventually your perineum (the tissue between your vagina and anus) will bulge and your baby's scalp will become visible.

- This moment can sting or burn quite a lot as the skin of your vagina stretches. This is normal and doesn't mean anything is wrong.

- Your midwife or doctor may ask you to push more slowly or gently, or to stop and pant until the urge to push has passed. This is to ensure a slow passage through the vagina, which reduces the risk of tearing.

- You will continue to push and eventually the baby's head will 'crown'. This is where the widest part of their head is visible.

DO YOU WANT BABY CLEANED UP AND HANDED TO YOU?

DO YOU WANT THE CORD CUT? IF SO BY WHOM?

Third stage of labour: Delivery of the placenta

- Delivery of the placenta usually takes 5–10 minutes.

- If possible, try to put your baby to your breast now as this triggers the release of oxytocin, which encourages the contractions that will naturally push out the placenta (physiological delivery).

- If your uterus isn't firm and contracting, you may be given an injection of syntometrine to assist the delivery of the placenta (managed delivery). Some midwives and doctors will automatically give you this injection.

DO YOU WANT A MANAGED THIRD STAGE OR A PHYSIOLOGICAL THIRD STAGE?

Pain Relief for Labour and Birth

Epidural

An epidural delivers continuous pain relief to the lower part of your body while allowing you to remain fully conscious. Medication is delivered through a catheter, a very thin, flexible, hollow tube that's inserted into the space just outside the membrane that surrounds your spinal cord and spinal fluid. The medication is usually a combination of a local anaesthetic and a narcotic. Local anaesthetics block sensations of pain, touch, movement and temperature, and narcotics blunt pain without affecting your ability to move your legs. Used together, they provide good pain relief with less loss of sensation in your legs and at a lower total dose than you'd need with just one or the other. An epidural is the most commonly used pain relief method in the United States.

PROS

☺ An epidural provides a route for very effective pain relief that can be used throughout your labour. If you are an Aspie who is hypersensitive to pain, this could be a good method of pain management for you.

☺ The anaesthetist can control the effects by adjusting the type, amount and strength of the medication. This is important because as your labour progresses and your baby moves further down into your birth canal, the dose you've been getting might no longer cover the pain.

☺ Since the effect of the medication is localised, you'll be awake and alert during labour and birth. And, because you're pain-free, you can rest if you want (or even sleep!) as your cervix dilates.

☺ Unlike other methods of pain relief, only a tiny amount of medication reaches your baby.

☺ Once the epidural is in place, it can be used to provide anaesthesia if you need a C-section.

CONS

☹ You have to stay in an awkward position for 10–15 minutes while the epidural is put in, and then wait another 5–20 minutes before the medication takes full effect. This may seem like a minor inconvenience, though, when you get hours of pain relief.

☹ Depending on the type and amount of medication you're getting, you may lose some sensation in your legs and be unable to stand. Many practitioners and hospitals won't allow you to get out of bed once you've had an epidural, whether you think you can walk or not.

☹ An epidural requires that you have an intravenous drip (IV), frequent blood pressure monitoring, and continuous foetal monitoring.

☹ An epidural often makes the pushing stage of labour longer. The loss of sensation in your lower body weakens your bearing-down reflex, which can make it harder for you to push your baby out.

☹ Having an epidural can make it more likely that you'll have a vacuum extraction or forceps delivery, which in turn increases your risk of tearing. The assistance of a vacuum or forceps also increases the risk of bruising for your baby. (The risks of more serious problems for your baby are relatively low.)

☹ In some cases, an epidural provides 'spotty' pain relief. This can happen because of variations in anatomy from one woman to the next, or if the medication doesn't manage to bathe all of your spinal nerves as it spreads through your epidural space.

☹ The catheter can also 'drift' slightly, making pain relief spotty after starting out fine.

☹ The drugs used in your epidural may temporarily lower your blood pressure, reducing blood flow to your baby, which in turn slows their heart rate.

☹ Anaesthetics delivered through an epidural can make it more difficult to tell when you need to pee. Also, if you can't pee into a bedpan, which for many people is harder than letting go on a toilet, you may need to be catheterised (have a catheter inserted into your urethra).

☹ In 1 in 100 women, an epidural causes a bad headache that may last for days. This is caused by a leakage of spinal fluid. (You can reduce the risk of headache by lying as still as possible while the needle is being positioned.)

☹ In very rare cases, an epidural affects breathing, and in extremely rare cases it causes nerve injury or infection.

Spinal block

How is a spinal block different from an epidural? Well it differs in two ways: First, it's delivered directly into the spinal fluid (rather than into the space just outside the membrane that surrounds the spinal fluid). Second, it's a one-off injection rather than a continuous feed through a catheter. As a result, relief is rapid and complete but lasts only a few hours. Your practitioner may order a spinal block if you decide you want pain relief late in labour or if you're progressing so quickly that birth is likely to be relatively soon and so you can't wait for an epidural.

You may feel some stinging when the medicine is first injected into the site, but the spinal block itself doesn't hurt. You may feel pressure, though, and as the spinal block starts working you'll feel numbness and loss of movement in your feet, then your legs, up to your waist. As the medication wears off, you'll regain the ability to move.

How numb you are depends on the medication used. A spinal performed during advanced labour may allow you to feel your contractions and move around in bed, while a spinal performed for a C-section will make you completely numb below the belly button and unable to move your legs.

PROS

☺ Complete pain relief kicks in after only a few minutes.

☺ Only a tiny amount of medication passes through to your baby.

CONS

☹ You have to stay in an awkward position, like you do with an epidural, for 5–10 minutes during the procedure.

☹ You need an IV and continuous foetal monitoring. Depending on the medication, you may or may not maintain muscle strength, which means you may or may not be able to walk about, even with assistance. Most midwives and doctors will want you to stay in bed once you've had a spinal block.

☹ The reduced sensation may make it harder for you to push your baby out, which can make the pushing stage longer and increase your chances of needing a vacuum extraction or forceps delivery, which in turn increases your risk of tearing.

☹ The drugs may temporarily lower your blood pressure, reducing blood flow to your baby, which in turn slows his heart rate.

☹ In rare cases, a spinal block causes an uncomfortable tingling sensation in your legs or buttocks that can last a couple of days.

☹ The spinal block can cause some soreness for a few days at the site of the injection.

☹ In 1 per cent of women, a spinal block causes a bad headache that may last for days.

☹ In very rare cases, a spinal block affects breathing, and in extremely rare cases it causes nerve injury or infection.

Gas and air (Entonox®)

This is commonly used in the United Kingdom for managing labour pain. The gas and air is breathed through a tube or a mask. It is made up of a 50:50 mixture of nitrous oxide and oxygen. It takes 20–30 seconds to take effect. It takes most women a few contractions to get the hang of it, so don't give up after one contraction. It makes you feel light-headed, so although it doesn't remove the pain, it makes you less aware of it.

PROS

☺ You control when and how deeply you breathe, and the effects wear off once you stop inhaling. I found this useful because I was in control. Control is very important for those of us on the autism spectrum, so you may find this is a good method if it is available to you.

CONS

☹ It may make you feel sick and light-headed to begin with. This tends to pass once you get used to it.

Pethidine (opiate)

This strong morphine-like analgesic is given by injection. It doesn't alter the pain as it is not an anaesthetic. Other opiates such as meptid, diamorphine and morphine may be offered, depending on where you are geographically.

PROS

☺ Pethidine changes your awareness and may help you to relax.

CONS

☹ You can't control it. Once you've had the injection, the effects last for up to four hours, so if you don't like the sensation you can't do anything about it. Nobody explained this to me and I had no idea until researching this book that pethidine doesn't alter the pain but can make you feel 'out of it'. If you don't know this and you have never experienced the sensation of taking an opiate, this may be one to avoid – especially if you are hypersensitive to any kind of drug.

☹ Pethidine passes through to your baby and can make babies slower to breathe at birth. If you take pethidine, your baby may also stay sleepy for several days, making breastfeeding harder to establish.

☹ For mums, pethidine may make you feel out of control, and make you feel sick. Opiates vary in their effectiveness and the extent to which they may make you feel sick.

General anaesthetic

This will be given to you by an anaesthetist (a specially trained doctor). It will either be given as a liquid that's injected into your veins through a cannula (a thin, plastic tube that feeds into a vein, usually on the back of your hand) or gas that you breathe in through a mask. The anaesthetist will stay with you throughout the procedure. They will monitor you to make sure you continue to receive the anaesthetic and you stay asleep, in a controlled state of unconsciousness. After the procedure, the anaesthetist will turn off the anaesthetic and you will gradually wake up.

PROS

☺ You are unconscious for the procedure which can help if you are highly anxious.

☺ You are unaware of the procedure taking place which can be frightening for some people.

CONS

☹ You will miss your baby being born as you will need to recover from the anaesthetic.

☹ A general anaesthetic has more complications associated with it.

Local anaesthetic

A local anaesthetic may also be required if you have had a large tear or episiotomy. This will be administered by injection into the perineum prior to the baby's head being delivered. You may also be given another injection of local anaesthetic prior to being stitched up.

Please note: I am not advocating any particular type of pain relief. What I am doing is giving information. If you are informed, then you have choice and you know what to expect. Those of us on the autism spectrum need this information.